WITHDRAWN
FROM STOCK

Coláiste Oideachais Mhuire Gan Smal
Luimneach

KU-190-463

Educational sciences

The history of education today

Antoine Léon

Prepared for the
International Bureau
of Education

In the series 'Educational sciences':

Landsheere, G. De. *Empirical research in education.* 1982, 113p.

Zverev, I.D. *Teaching methods in the Soviet school.* 1983, 116p.

Kraevskij, V.V.; Lerner, I.Y. *The theory of curriculum content in the USSR.* 1984. 113p.

Léon, Antoine. *The history of education today.* 1985. 117p.

Coláiste
Mhuire Gan Smal
Luimneach

Class No.	370.9
Suffix	
Acc. No.	1240365
BRN	86941

Published by the United Nations
Educational, Scientific and Cultural Organization,
7, place de Fontenoy, 75700 Paris, France.

ISBN: 92-3-102271-7

Printed in the United Kingdom by
Richard Clay (The Chaucer Press) Ltd, Bungay, Suffolk

© Unesco 1985

Preface

By devoting a monograph in its 'Educational sciences' series to the history of education, the International Bureau of Education has sought to draw the attention of teachers, research specialists and educational policy makers to the evolution of this field in the context of the development of the various educational sciences. Moving from the history of events to the comparative history of educational doctrines, institutions, practices and techniques, this discipline enables us both to assess the progress achieved by the various educational sciences and to see how they have become interlinked in the course of their development. At the same time, it highlights a trend toward the universalization of problems, and this leads at least to common questions about them, though not perhaps to a uniformity of solutions to them. These common questions, while they are justified by the growing impact of scientific and technological progress on all aspects of peoples' life, introduce a new manner of perceiving and apprehending interdependencies – horizontal as well as vertical – between the various education systems throughout the world and throughout periods of time. What other discipline could better train minds, as the century draws to a close, to grasp the notion of relativity between situations and that of solidarity between generations and peoples, while establishing a rational basis for their cultural identity? And what other discipline could provide a better foundation for philosophical reflection or for a futurological approach to education, by establishing the primacy of the universal over the singular since the remotest past, and perhaps never more than today when frontiers are giving way, whether they be frontiers in time and space retreating before the development of modern communication media or cultural and linguistic frontiers which are also rapidly disappearing as a result of educational progress? While the importance of this discipline as well as its place among the educational sciences is abundantly clear, the difficulty of presenting all its facets within the necessarily constraining dimensions of a monograph such as the present one is in the nature of a challenge; and it is indeed no small merit on the part of Professor A. Léon not only to have overcome this difficulty but to have extended to us such an eminently readable invitation to reflect effectively on the questions raised by a discipline which is so often, and mistakenly, considered as being thoroughly conventional and oriented towards the past.

While reiterating our thanks to Professor Antoine Léon for his valuable contribution to this new series of monographs, we would remind our readers that the ideas and opinions expressed in this work are those of the author and do not necessarily represent the views of Unesco. Moreoever, the designations employed and the presentation of the material throughout the publication do not imply the expression of any opinion whatsoever on the part of Unesco concerning the legal status of any country, territory, city or area or of its authorities, or concerning the delimitations of its frontiers or boundaries.

Contents

Introduction

One outcome of the substantial increase in studies on the history of education over the past two decades has been the founding of the International Association for the History of Education. Under its 1979 by-laws, one of its main objectives is to sponsor the development of research, encourage exchanges between researchers and bring out the proper place that should be assigned to the history of education in training programmes.

The study and application of this broad discipline is not the sole preserve of research specialists: a number of 'outsiders' are quite rightly, but with varying degrees of success, trying to set subjects they study or teach in their historical context.

Different people assign different individual or social functions to the history of education. What these functions are and, more concretely, how interesting and useful they rate studying the history of education depend on the image they have of this discipline, how they represent its purpose and scope and the themes and approaches it features and, in a more general way, how they conceive of the relationship between past and present.

Accordingly, before setting out to define the functions of the history of education, it seems necessary to reflect on the nature of the history referred to.

One aim of the present study is to draw from the analysis of recent works and compile elements of information, reflections and discussion related to the current state of the history of education.

In this respect the richness, diversity and in many cases novelty of the themes covered have come together to make a whole that is apt to meet the expectations of all those involved in teaching. Further, to the extent that they focus on the analysis of the connection between education and social change, historians shed new light on the matter and elicit fresh questioning on how the education system actually works and how it is responding to the various crises it is undergoing.

In other words, studies on the history of education will be consistently more apposite in providing answers to the questions raised by teachers, administrators, researchers and students about what will become of the school as an institution and about the meaningfulness of their own work.

These preliminary remarks give some indication of the arrangement of this book by subject-matter.

Part One will take stock of 'the history of education today', presenting its scope and orientations. It will be introduced by a brief review of how the discipline has evolved and will be concluded by some reflections on its place among the human sciences.

Part Two deals with the factors and mechanisms of change in education. This fundamental question will be broached through analysing more concrete themes such as the history of literacy and of folk culture, and the development of technical education.

The more direct study, in Part Three, of the functions of the history of education will lead on to the outlining of a few principles related to teacher training and the teaching of history to students.

A final section contains some thoughts on what the history of education can mean to us.

To conclude this introduction, we should like to define the bounds of this study. They are of two types: the first has to do with the choice of themes, the examples submitted and the conceptions which are analysed or criticized; the second relates to the amount and geographical spread of the underlying documentation.

It was out of the question for us to put together a comprehensive survey of all the subjects to which specialists of all countries are addressing themselves in their study of the history of education.

True, the bulk of examples given, in particular in the second section (Chapters V and VI) are drawn from the history of education in France, but as far as possible we have referred to available documentation in our discussion of the situation in other countries. Whatever the case, whether it be a matter of France, the other industrialized countries or the Third World, the examples are only intended to illustrate conceptions, trends, mechanisms or fairly general factors. More specifically, the similarity or convergence of research content allows us to feel that the pertinence of the information and reflections contained in this book will extend beyond the individual works and countries it covers.

In this respect, we wish to thank all those who were so good as to reply to the requests for information we sent out to them. We also extend out thanks to the various colleagues who gave us the benefit of their remarks and suggestions at meetings organized by the International Bureau of Education.

PART ONE

The history of education today

CHAPTER I

The growth of the history of education

The 1960s: a turning-point

The experts of many countries agree that the beginning of the 1960s was a key period in the evolution of the history of education.

In the United States, according to W.W. Brickman, this period began with the recognition of two phenomena: a reduction in the number of theses on the history of education, and the lesser importance given to this discipline in teacher training programmes. The period was also characterized by the emergence of the revisionist or radical movement[1]. In the view of this movement's proponents, the development of public education in the course of the nineteenth century, far from having helped to build up American democracy, had primarily served as an instrument of domination and control to the benefit of the middle and upper classes.

In order to show how rapidly ideas relating to the history of education have evolved in the course of the last two decades, J.D. Wilson compares three books published respectively in 1957, 1970 and 1975. The first, entitled *The development of education in Canada* by C.E. Phillips, and written in a democratic and egalitarian spirit, favours the growth of the public education system and contrasts the action of the 'good' reformers, in other words those of the liberal tradition, to the resistance put up by the 'evil' conservatives. In addition, the author tends to play down disputes over educational matters except in the case of tension between the State and the various churches. Thirteen years later, a work edited by J.D. Wilson and entitled *Canadian education: the history*, cited recent research as its authority in linking the history of education to social history and in advancing theories similar to those of the American revisionists. Finally, the third work, *Education and social change: themes from Ontario's past* by M.B. Katz and P.H. Mattingly, was openly revisionist[2].

In France, according to R. Chartier, the advent of the 'new history' of education marks the passage from institutional, ideological or monographic history to a new approach based on the joint efforts of historians and sociologists[3]. To take an example, the latter set out to analyse the complex relations linking scholastic institutions to the structures of society, thus at the same time giving substance to new concepts such as the cultural inheritance or the equalization of opportunity, and new themes such as the influence of students' origin on the length of studies, on the rate of success in qualifying for diplomas, or on social mobility. How are we to account for this rather rapid change of orientations and programme areas in the history of education?

The misadventures of historiography

The writing of history has its own history. Since we lack space here to consider the contributions of the pioneers such as Herodotes, Thucydides or, nearer to our own time, Ibn Khaldun, or the contributions of various philosophic doctrines to the formulation of historiography, we will confine ourselves to the changes which took place during the Renaissance in the approach of historians to the past.

The contribution of Herodotes and Thucydides is discussed in Chapter VIII. As regards Ibn Khaldun (1332–1406), his fundamental contribution to the development of scientific history (i.e. one in which all sources are checked and several series of factors are taken into account) in no way obscures the value of his reflections on educational problems, such as those relating to regional disparities, the origin of intellectual inequalities, or the professionalization of the teaching function[4].

A century later two historians, G. Monod[5] and K. Pomian[6], considered these changes to be due to the rapid transformations characteristic of this period, the acceleration of history making possible a new interest and new attitudes with regard to the past. 'If the historical sense was to develop,' Monod wrote in this respect, 'the past had to appear quite distinct from the present, so that it could be studied objectively and as it were from a distance. [In the course of the Renaissance] the difference between the Middle Ages and the present was obvious to all, so that people took a completely fresh interest in the study of the past'[7]. Pomian, for his part, analysing changes in the approach to historiography, emphasizes the passage from immediate knowledge, in which the historian is simply a recorder accepting the testimony of eye-witnesses or the repositories of tradition, to mediate knowledge in which the historian's point of view tends to become independent of that of persons who lived during the period under examination. In other words, the intelligible is not the immediately visible. 'Faith,' states Pomian, 'is the only road that reason has found to arrive at knowledge of invisible and partly unknowable things. To make an act of faith is to admit the authority of someone who has seen something that I have not seen myself. It is to give him my confidence and accept his account literally'[8].

This change from immediate to mediate knowledge is associated with a transformation of the representation of time. The former cyclical conception of time was not such as to provoke any new approach, inasmuch as it led the historian to seek in the past patterns similar to those of the present. By contrast, the new rectilinear and cumulative conception of time confronts the historian with entirely novel problems, forcing him to find appropriate methods and techniques to construct his theory. The cyclical notion of time appears as a source of intellectual laziness. The rectilinear notion, which is more demanding, implies the idea of progress. The spread of this idea to all aspects of human activity occurred in the eighteenth century.

It goes without saying that this change of historiographical approach is far from being absolute in so far as the study of certain cultures obliges the historian to make use of the oral testimony of those who act as depositories of tradition or of collective memory; but this necessity in no way excuses the historian from preserving a critical attitude to such testimony or from attempting an intelligible reconstruction of the past.

In the course of recent decades, the rapid transformation of all the conditions of life has made it necessary to take a new look at the past. The decline of Europe, from a demographic, cultural (stemming from a general recognition of the diversity of civilizations) and political (as a result of decolonization) standpoint, has called the products of traditional historiography, centred as they are on the past of the Western nations, into question[9]. In addition, the importance attributed to economic factors or the action of the masses, and the development of sciences relating to human beings and society, have enlarged the field of historiography and caused new research instruments to emerge. Among these may be mentioned the use of fiscal documents, school registries and manuals, and the employment of statistical techniques[10].

As regards the evolution of the history of education, American specialists consider that the break which occurred in the 1960s was due less to an increase in curiosity with regard to the past than to a development of interest in present problems. In other words, in the climate of international competition which existed at the end of the 1950s – when the usual forms of international competition (i.e. economic, military and ideological) were sharpened by new rivalries arising from the launching of the first satellites – and on the basis of research into the teaching given at that time, the need to work out a national education policy led to the development of faulty theories of historical approach[11]. This tendency to 'presentism', in other words the projection of present-day problems on to the past, may be ascribed to the meeting or collaboration – from which the revisionist movement sprang – between historians of education and social scientists[12].

What are the main contributions of this new version of the history of education?

The 'new history' and criticism of the school as an institution

In taking up new subjects and changing orientations, the historiography of education displays a trend which started well before the beginning of the 1960s. In this respect, one may recall the works of the Belgian Henri Pirenne, a specialist in the economic, social and demographic history of the Middle Ages; of Huizinga, the Dutch historian of mentalities; and of the Polish historian Znaniecki, who drew upon popular autobiographical accounts. Most frequently, however, the principal source of the renewal of historiography[13] is seen as the *Ecole des Annales*, founded in 1929 by Lucien Febvre and Marc Bloch.

In the course of the 1970s, various French historians claiming to take their inspiration from the *Ecole des Annales* movement or, more generally, that of the 'new history', took up and systematized some of the tendencies which had surfaced during the preceding decades. These trends, which have undoubtedly influenced the work of educational historians[14], may be summed up as follows:

— The enlargement of the historian's field of interest. 'Total history', advocated by Febvre, takes account of different streams such as economic, social and psychological history, and concerns itself equally with the most distant past and with the present.

— The tendency for narrative history to be replaced by 'theme history'. According to this new approach, one should study the object before beginning to collect or analyse the texts. 'It is the problem area which gives rise to the sources, which are practically inexhaustible'[15].

— The break-up and expansion of the purely documentary approach. To written, iconographical or archaeological testimony are added the oral accounts of the last witnesses of vanished customs or, in the case of recent history, visual or auditive recording. In addition, the historian nowadays takes an interest in 'imaginary documents', by which we mean the idea which people in the past had of reality, and in 'the silences of history'. In this respect, is it not true that the peoples said to be without any history are rather those peoples about whose history we are ignorant[16]?

— A certain desire to escape from the apparent one-dimensional approach to the evolution of events and to place more emphasis on conflict and on the phenomena of anticipation and persistence which punctuate or form a structure with their evolution.

— The simultaneous taking into account of short- and long-term phenomena. This makes it possible to make an inventory of the various effects (the productive and repetitively productive function) which can be ascribed to education[17], and to accede to a certain kind of wisdom (see the conclusion to this book).

— The tendency to accord as much weight to the personality of the witness or to the conditions
in which the testimony was produced as to its content.

— The realization that the work of the historian and the products of historiography are relative.

'Yes,' writes Paul Veyne in this connection, 'history is no more than a reply to our questions because we are not able to ask all the possible questions or to describe the whole process of evolution, and because the progress of historical enquiry is placed in time and is as slow as that of any science. Yes, history is subjective because one cannot deny that the choice of subjects for a history book is free' [18]. No doubt it is true that the work of the historian is to a considerable extent subjective, whether in the choice of subjects or in the manner of interrogating in the past. In such choice and such interrogation, the general and specific culture of the historian, his opinions and his personality play an important part. But surely the requirements of objectivity are or should be satisfied when it is no longer a matter of asking questions but of replying in the most precise and rigorous way possible on the basis of a systematic exploitation of available resources.

In the United States, the notion of the 'new history' is assimilated to the revisionist movement which considers teaching as a substitute for the family, the church and the community, traditional institutions whose authority is in constant decline. Put another way, the school thus becomes responsible for the maintenance of national cohesion and the inculcation of codes and values calculated to ensure stability and social order [19]. While calling into question what Lawrence Cremin calls 'the narrowly institutional approach', the revisionists, in view of the unfavourable situation in which immigrants and ethnic minorities are currently placed, condemn the conservative nature of school reforms and emphasize the closeness of the links between education, political relations and social structures[20]. Analysis of the functions of the school also leads them to raise precise questions concerning recruitment (for example the sex, age, ethnic origin and social level of pupils), the number of years of education, the school or university routes followed, and the individual or social effects of education. Revisionists' interest in the problems of literacy extends beyond the frontiers of the United States. It also leads them to raise questions regarding the aims of the school policy of the Western powers in their former colonies, and whether it was oriented towards liberation or integration.

One of the significant contributions of the 'new history', whether European or American, is the overthrow of the chronological framework normally used by historians and, by the same token, the recognition of the importance of hitherto neglected periods. For example, far from being limited to the nineteenth century, the process of conveying literacy to the lower classes of the population goes back to the sixteenth century. Throughout the intervening period, the teaching of reading and writing was mainly carried on outside the school by the church and the local community.

All this calling into question, however, has not failed to provoke reactions.

Not all the harm comes from the school

The dominant preoccupations of contemporary historiography in no way obscure the persistence of apparently traditional themes of an institutional or doctrinal kind, which are still able to inspire fresh views of the past.

However that may be, any aspect of the history of education currently in vogue cannot be an entirely new discovery. Thus, in his *Histoire de la pédagogie*, published in 1886, Gabriel Compayré considered that this discipline 'in its vast scope, should embrace the entire field of intellectual and moral culture of all ages and all countries'[21]. He went on to add that, in addition to formal education, there exists 'a natural education that one receives unawares, without volition, through the influence of the social surroundings in which one lives. There exists what a contemporary philosopher has cleverly called the occult co-workers in education, i.e. climate, race, customs, social condition, political institutions and religious beliefs.' Further on, under the name of auxiliary agents of education, he mentions the influence of books, 'both bad and good', which, in his view, are dangerous rivals to what he considers the indispensable role of the school.

This role, contested by the revisionists and by the most obdurate defenders of the 'new history', has been the object of a critical re-examination on the part of what are called the 'post-revisionists'. In this connection, C.J. Lucas proposes the adoption of a position half-way between the 'cynicism' of the revisionists and the optimism of those who see in the school the irreplaceable instrument of the development of American democracy. He backs up this point of view with an analysis of well-defined socio-cultural themes such as autonomy, job mobility or the integration of ethnic minorities. In his opinion, in each of these cases there is a need to underline the ambiguity of the role of the school and to draw a distinction between the intentions behind certain measures and their real effects. Thus, 'to admit that the school may have been able to play a role in the control of thought does not mean that it has destroyed individual independence of the freedom of thought'[22].

Elsewhere, Lucas, like C. Webster, denounces the abuse of 'presentism' in the work of the revisionists. In his view, this abuse leads them, on the one hand, to exaggerate the similarities relative to the differences between periods which are far removed from one another and, on the other, to use the past in the defence of a modern cause[23]. For his part, M. Greene considers exaggerated the picture which the revisionists draw of a social control invariably exercised in a negative sense on individuals portrayed as passive and malleable. In this connection he emphasizes one of the paradoxes underlying all educational action, namely that in order to acquire or preserve a sense of identity a person needs a framework, an outline and a form that social control makes it easier to define. In other words, situated as it is at the meeting point of the demands of society and the search for independence, the only way forward for education is to embrace the very conflict which simultaneously opposes and links these two forces [24].

Brickman's criticisms are aimed more particularly at the methodological weaknesses in the work of the revisionist historians. In his view, they under-estimate the place of erudition, lack rigour in their application of the rules of historiography and are guilty of hasty generalizations[25]. This criticism seems the more worthy of attention in that many pseudo-historians, ignoring the requirements of documentary research, do not take much trouble to distin-guish, in their conclusions, between what stems from carefully checked sources of information and what is in effect interpretation or mere imagina-tion.

Without explicitly attacking the revisionist movement, M. Agulhon examines the criticisms frequently expressed regarding the primary school of Jules Ferry. These criticisms can be gathered under four headings: under the Third Republic, the primary school was simultaneously the school of social docility and conformity; the school of the class system, reproducing social partitions; the school of chauvinism, nationalism and colonial imperialism; and, finally, the school of national uniformity via the 'cultural genocide' of the 'less French' regions[26].

This is how Agulhon puts the nature and scope of the last of the above-mentioned criticisms into a different perspective.

In the first place, 'the State in its present form had already existed for one or two centuries when the Third Republic inherited it, and this inheritance already comprised common institutions and the use of one language of public communication. If there is something wrong with that, it would be fairer to blame the far-off monarchist founders of the system . . .' Furthermore, it is by no means proved that this republican urge to make the French language universally known was in fact accompanied by any desire to eliminate the other languages or dialects . . . In the last resort, the decline of regional languages and cultures stems from causes which have no direct relation with educational policy. In effect, 'regional cultures, unless they are deliberately and militantly kept up, fade away with the destruction of traditional rural life . . ., with the complete opening up of agriculture to the national and international market, with the advent of the modern mass media of which the standardizing power, or let us say quite simply the power, is much greater than that of the education system.' In a word, 'Jules Ferry cannot simultaneously be the scapegoat for all the sins of the Capetians and those of the television companies. He is too recent for the first and too ancient for the second . . . He should be judged in relation to his own time and to the intention behind his work'[27].

It is commonplace to blame the present crisis of French education on the difficulties experienced by the system in embodying the functions and values (the reinforcement of national unity and the reduction of social inequality) formerly advocated by the associates of Jules Ferry.

However, one cannot blame the system for calling these functions and values into question, or for their decline. In this connection, René Rémond claims that the education crisis 'has its origin and its roots anywhere other than in education: it is essentially a reflection of the crisis of society itself, calling into question our civilization and its values, and our political system'. Thus he considers that it will only find 'its solution and its outcome within a general framework involving society, culture and democracy as a whole'[28].

Needless to say, the worsening of this crisis casts light on certain attitudes of the architects of the 'new history' and reveals the emergence of new themes in the field of the history of education.

NOTES AND REFERENCES

1. Brickman, W.W. Theoretical and critical perspectives on educational history. *Paedagogica historica* (Ghent, Belgium), vol. XVIII, no. 1, 1978, p. 42–83.
2. Wilson, J.D. Historiographical perspectives on Canadian educational history: a review essay. *The journal of educational thought* (Calgary, Alta., Faculty of Education, University of Calgary), vol. 11, no. 1, 1977, p. 49–63.
3. Chartier, R. Education. *In:* Le Goff, J., ed. *La nouvelle histoire.* Paris, Retz, 1978, p. 156–158.
4. Ibn Khaldun. *Ibn Khaldun – the Muqaddimah: an introduction to history.* Transl. by Franz Rosenthal. 2nd ed. Princeton, NJ, Princeton University Press, 1967. 1700 p.
5. Monod, J. Du progrès des études historiques en France depuis le XVIe siècle. *Revue historique* (Paris), no. 1, 1876 (Article reproduced in issue no. 518, 1976, of the same journal, p. 297–324).
6. Pomian, K. L'histoire de la science et l'histoire de l'histoire. *Annales* (Paris), no. 5, 1975, p. 935–952.
7. Monod, J. *Op. cit.*
8. Pomian, K. *Op. cit.*
9. Furet, F. *L'atelier de l'histoire.* Paris, Flammarion, 1982. 320 p.
10. Carbonell, C.-O. *L'historiographie.* Paris, Presses universitaires de France, 1981. 128 p.
11. Webster, C. Changing perspectives in the history of education. *Oxford review of education* (Oxford, United Kingdom), vol. 2, no. 3, 1976, p. 201–213.
12. Graff, H.J. 'The new math': quantification, the 'new' history and the history of education. *Urban education* (Beverly Hills, CA), vol. 11, no. 4, January 1977, p. 403–440.
13. Carbonell, C.-O. *Op. cit.*
14. Léon, A. *Introduction à l'histoire des faits éducatifs.* Paris, Presses universitaires de France, 1980. 248 p.
15. Carbonell, C.-O. *Op. cit.*
16. Veyne, P. *Comment on écrit l'histoire.* Paris, Seuil, 1971. 352 p.
17. Petitat, A. *Production de l'école. Production de la société.* Geneva, Librairie Droz, 1982. 540 p.
18. Veyne, P. *Op. cit.*
19. Greene, M. Identities and contours: an approach to educational history. *Educational researcher* (Washington, DC, American Educational Research Association), vol. 2, no. 4, April 1973, p. 5–10.
20. Ibid.
21. Compayré, G. *Histoire de la pédagogie.* Paris, Delaplane, 1886.
22. Lucas, C.J. Schooling and American life: in search of a post-revisionist interpretation. *Journal of thought* (Fayetteville, AR, University of Arkansas), vol. 10, no. 10, November 1975, p. 271–284.

23. Webster, C. *Op. cit.*, p. 201–213.
24. Greene, M. *Op. cit.*, p. 5–10.
25. Brickman, W.W. *Op. cit.*, p. 42–83.
26. Agulhon, M. Cent ans d'école primaire, laïque, gratuite et obligatoire: un bilan critique. *Les Cahiers rationalistes* (Paris, Union rationaliste), no. 371, 1981, p. 9–22.
27. Ibid.
28. Rémond, R. Préface. *In:* Parias, L.-H., ed. *Histoire générale de l'enseignment et de l'éducation en France.* Paris, Nouvelle Librairie de France, 1981, t. 1, p. 44.

CHAPTER II

The scope of
the history of education

An unfinished and unfinishable inventory

To determine the limits of the scope of history is no easy task. One might even go so far as to say, like P. Veyne[1], that this scope 'is completely indeterminate' inasmuch as 'everything is historical', every event is worth recording, and the writing of history, which now aims at becoming total, is now taking over different fields of knowledge such as economics, society, demography, or the attitudes of people.

However, if we keep strictly to the history of education, it is possible, like Brickman, to distinguish between two definitions of the scope of the subject, one narrow, the other broad[2]. The first is only concerned with certain institutional forms of conveying technology or knowledge, whereas the second embraces all types of influence, whether formal or informal, on individuals or groups. It takes into account not only the school, but also the family, the churches, means of communication, youth clubs, etc. In addition, it takes in all the factors and results of the process of the development of people in society: ideology, administration, finance, organization, the methods and content of education, the effects of educative action, etc.

Over and above these categories, the scope of the history of education could extend to all countries and all periods, including the present. The recently published *Histoire mondiale de l'éducation* seems to belong to this 'extensive' school of thought[3].

It is out of the question in this short chapter to draw up a systematic inventory of contemporary research into the history of education. Our more modest design is to show the diversity of subjects in which research workers in the history of education interest themselves. This will take two forms. First of all we shall mention the themes of recent international meetings and the research programmes of institutions specializing in the subject. To this end, we shall use the *International newsletter for the history of education*[4] and the results of an enquiry among the directors of research centres [5]. Second, we shall present some of the apparently dominant themes in the present field of the history of education, namely the organization and functioning of the school; educational instruments and aids; the recipients and the agents of education (among others women and teachers); and international comparisons and school policy in Third World countries during the colonial era.

Further themes, notably literacy, popular culture and technical education, will be considered in Part Two of the present publication which deals with the factors and mechanisms of change, and in Part Three, in relation to the functions of the teaching of history.

Side by side with the exploration or thorough investigation of these relatively recent themes, the study of more classical themes such as the history of an institution, the analysis of an educational movement or the interpretation of texts from earlier ages continues. There can be no question of establishing any kind of a hierarchy among these various studies. For example, the in-depth study of an educational work may call for the most refined forms of linguistic analysis or statistical treatment.

Diversity of themes and approaches

The general themes of the most recent conferences of the International Association for the History of Education serve to convey an idea of the scientific interests of educational historians in different countries: 'Teacher training' (Louvain, 1979); 'Educational innovations in a historical context' (Warsaw, 1980); 'Educational policies in their historical context: social, economic, political and cultural factors' (Paris, 1981); 'The history of pre-school education and its relations with the history of education in general' (Budapest, 1982); 'Science, technology and education' (Oxford, 1983).

In addition, national lists of current research projects and the programmes of meetings organized by national associations of the history of education reveal the diversity of the chosen themes in the different countries.

For its 1980 Annual Conference, the United States Society for the History of Education included the following topics, among others, in its programme[6]:

— the comparative history of literacy;
— the origin and evolution of social services for youth (1880–1980);
— American political education in the Federal Republic of Germany in the post-war period;
— iconographical aspects of the history of education;
— historical approaches to leadership in the field of school administration, etc.

It would seem that the major contributions of research workers in the United States in this field appear in the review *History of education quarterly*, founded in 1961.

In France, the History of Education Service of the *Institut national de recherche pédagogique* has been publishing the review *Histoire de l'éducation* since 1978. In its programme for the year 1981–82, the service recognizes three main fields of research[7].

Projects in the first category deal with the development of fundamental instruments of research such as a bibliography of the history of French education, a guide to sources (information of an archival type concerning technical education in particular) and an inventory of the educational patrimony (an enquiry into the schoolhouse in the nineteenth century). Projects in the second category are concerned with the compiling of two major lists, the first of schoolbooks and the second of the educational press. The latter, which has been published in part, constitutes an original working tool for all research workers. According to the authors, it may also, as a result of the study by series of thousands of journals, provide food for thought on the nature and evolution of the educational phenomenon[8]. Finally, the third research category covers the following three themes:

— colleges of the *ancien régime* (construction of the school network; social functioning of establishments; the diversification of educational networks);
— the history of the centralized administration of public education and of the general inspectorate;
— the history of academic disciplines. The function of this last theme is defined as follows: To bring out the factors of this evolution with a view to enabling educational research to take it into account in working out answers to questions raised by the present system of education; to contribute to the training of teachers by leading them to reflect on the historical character of disciplines which they would naturally tend to think of as 'eternal'.

In the United Kingdom, working groups of the History of Education Society are studying the following subjects: post-secondary education; confessional education; curricula; the education of women; physical education; and literacy. The themes of the two meetings organized by this association during 1982 were the place of the history of education in teacher training and the physical condition of the nation and health education in the nineteenth and twentieth centuries. Two journals, entitled *History of education* and *History of Education Society bulletin,* are to be the association's official publications. Another periodical, the *Oxford review of education,* calls for contributions from authors practising different disciplines in order to make possible more thorough treatment of complex themes such as the relationship between literacy and industrialization, or the degree of importance of family education throughout the course of history[9].

At the University of Ghent (Belgium), the *Centre pour l'études de l'histoire de l'éducation,* directed by K. de Clerck, publishes the review *Paedagogica historica,* founded in 1961 by R.L. Plancke with a view to 'laying the foundation for a general and comparative history of education and contributing to a better knowledge of the history of ideas and of educational institutions in various countries'. Among the research projects being carried out at the centre are the history of education, teaching and educational policy in Belgium since 1830; the history of primary school-teachers and their professional associations in Belgium in the course of the second half of the nineteenth century; and the history of women's education in Belgium since 1830. These projects derive from a general concept of education in teaching as being essentially social phenomena. The authors emphasize the recurrence of forms of behaviour throughout history.

The historical research projects of the Pedagogical Institute of the University of Zürich, under the leadership of F.P. Hager, are largely devoted to educational ideas and theories, and notably to the influence of Plato's ideas on the history of educational thought in Europe, for example on Comenius, Rousseau, Pestalozzi, Dilthey, and others. Analysis of the texts of these authors relates to philosophical and hermeneutic approaches.

In Warsaw, a group of research workers in the history of education has joined the Institute of the History of Science, Education and Technology, directed by J. Miaso. The group is working primarily on the role of education in the history of the Polish nation, or more specifically the formation of national culture during the periods when Poland was divided up among foreign powers; the social functions of higher education since the eighteenth century; adult education and the popularization of science in the nineteenth and twentieth centuries; the evolution of professional teaching; changes in the education system since the Second World War, and so on.

In Budapest, where the fourth conference of the International Association for the History of Education was held in 1982, O. Vág is the chairman of an international working group on the history of pre-school education. The members of this group appear to have a predominantly comparative approach.

In the USSR, research in the history of education is carried out partly at the Institute of Scientific Research on General Education of the Academy of Pedagogical Sciences, and partly in fifteen scientific research institutes grouped under the Union Republics. To these must be added the chairs of education in the universities and teachers' training colleges. Approximately 300 research workers are working in the field of the history of education.

The department of school history and teaching methods, at the Academy of Pedagogical Sciences, possesses three historical research units, dealing respectively with the pre-revolutionary period, the Soviet period and foreign countries. These units publish a series of studies on school history and educational thought pertaining to the different peoples who make up the USSR. The peculiarities of education in each Soviet Republic form the object of a historical study. Soviet historians attach value to and popularize the inheritance of great teachers of the past. They also study school history and educational thought in the market economy countries, drawing attention to the contribution of the international labour movement and to that of Marxist educationists in these countries. Finally, they take part in compiling an educational library for the benefit of teachers.

This short review of the activities of a few educational research centres gives no more than an incomplete picture of the extent and diversity of this academic discipline.

In a further exploration of this field, we are obliged to concentrate on some of the more common themes of recent research.

The building, functioning and aims of the school system

In this vast sector of the history of education, a number of very different contributions are being made, different by virtue both of their aims and of the time or space frame taken into account.

The inventory of colleges of the *ancien régime* has inspired M.-M. Compère and D. Julia[10] to a number of observations and reflections on the ways in which secondary education in France grew up. First of all, it is to be noted that the transition from the mediæval school to the modern college is characterized by the organization of hierarchically arranged classes, each with a teacher assigned to it, and by the allocation of buildings or premises specifically for the purpose of education. Second, the growing numbers of small provincial colleges, from the middle of the seventeenth century on, was a response to a growing demand for education, parallel to economic development, among the leading citizens of small towns, to family feeling (in the sense of wanting to keep children at home longer), and to local patriotism, the college becoming a means of cultural discrimination. Finally, the authors sketch out a geographical distribution of colleges on a regional basis, and seek reasons for the disparities observed. In Brittany, for example, the inadequate number of colleges is ascribed, among other causes, to administrative shortcomings, to a shortage of tertiary functions and to the fact that writing was rarely used in local rural society.

Analysing the curriculum and orientation of pupils in colleges under the *ancien régime*, W. Frijhoff and D. Julia[11] would appear to confirm the theories of certain sociologists regarding the school's function of reproducing the class system. However, this function was carried out in a manner specific to the period under examination. While the colleges did admit considerable numbers of children from modest backgrounds, many of the latter dropped out before the end of the educational cycle in order to carry on their father's trade or, at the best, to enter the clergy.

The regulations for the construction of colleges and school architecture in general always express a certain concept of the organization of education and a certain picture of the public concerned[12]. The same applies to the drawing of the school map. Thus the desire frequently expressed during the second half of the eighteenth century to rationalize the drawing of such maps arose, in the opinion of Julia, 'from the desire, based on progress in political arithmetic, to govern people by means of figures'[13]. More precisely, it was a matter of assigning a territory to each university with a view to immobilizing the 'wandering dunces' and of trying to improve the quality of devalued diplomas 'by putting a stop to the fruitful speculations of unscrupulous professors'. It was also a question of 'establishing a school network strictly ranked from top to bottom, laid out on the ground according to the demographic and economic logic of urban distribution'.

The strictly pedagogical organization of nineteenth century primary schools (e.g. as regards teaching methods, use of time, the grouping of pupils and the separation of sexes) has recently been the object of in-depth study[14].

Teacher/pupil relations within the classroom itself have been studied by J. Contou in a thesis on punishment in the nineteenth century secondary schools[15]. In this work, the author investigated, among other things, factors such as the weight and rigidity of the hierarchical system, the relative immobility of poorly qualified staff, and the persistence of an outdated view of the child, which might throw light on the nature of teacher/pupil relations.

Such relations develop through the means of transmitting and testing knowledge. In this connection, teaching methods and the content of education have been the subject of a number of research projects[16], notably as regards the teaching of history. In the case of certain subjects, the evolution of content and form is closely linked to political and economic history. This is the case with the teaching of political economy in the nineteenth century. This discipline was the object of a number of measures tending to reduce its importance. In 1819 it was taught under the name of industrial economics only at the *Conservatoire des arts et métiers*, in other words well away from all the major establishments of public education. In 1830, the creation of a chair of political economy at the *Collège de France* stemmed from the same desire to screen off the subject, inasmuch as this deliberately theoretical course was only intended for a minority of students. Several years earlier, by contrast, an ordinance had laid down that faculties of law, open to a wider public, should only purvey 'positive and usual knowledge'. Not before the 1860s, with the liberalization of the imperial regime and the triumph of free trade, were genuine courses of political economy to be given in faculties of law[17].

Educative action and the transmission of knowledge are carried out by means of aids and instruments, the evolution of which represents a relatively new branch of the history of education[18].

Aids and instruments in education and teaching

We will confine ourselves here to three categories of material: schoolbooks, audio-visual aids and toys.

According to the estimates of Alain Choppin, taking all subjects and levels

into account[19], there have been about 100,000 different French school-books since the Revolution. The historical study of such manuals is doubly interesting in that, according to this author, they represent not only a struc-ture of knowledge but an instrument of power. As a structure, manuals impose a division and a classification of knowledge, thus helping to construct the pupils' intellectual framework. As an instrument of power, books con-tribute to a linguistic uniformity, to cultural levelling and to the propagation of the dominant ideas. With its multi-faceted nature, the schoolbook is sub-ject to different historical approaches. In effect, it can be studied as an arte-fact, as a teaching tool and as a structuring of knowledge. It can also be looked at from a political point of view, in the light of constraining or liberal legislation, thus giving rise to comparative research.

Less well known than that of schoolbooks, the history of audio-visual aids cannot, in the opinion of J. Perriault, be restricted to a simple account of technical devices ranging from the magic lantern and the gramophone to the tape-recorder. It should take into account the social function of these objects and analyse the gap between the logic of the inventor and that of the user[20]. For example, the magic lantern, which was invented around 1640, was seen by its inventors as a means both of instruction and of amusement. In the eighteenth century, however, it was viewed simply as a fairground attraction. It would seem not to have been appreciated as a teaching aid until the nineteenth century, as an answer to needs created by industrialization and as a result of the competition between Church and State for the control of youth.

Over and above its immediate effects as a teaching aid or source of plea-sure, 'the magic lantern left its mark on the societies where it became common, the most obvious sign of which is the habit of gathering together in the evening in order to see a show'. It also 'in the long term helped to create that consumer market for the imaginary which is such a dominant feature of the world we live in today'. Thus Perriault proposes 'to cross the history of peddling or of the movement for popular education with that of the sudden appearance of the magic lantern project or the gramophone project'.

The subject of C. Thollon-Pommerol[21] is somewhat different, since the author seeks to consider teaching by means of the image in relation with other factors such as the development of projection apparatus. The history of teach-ing by visual image reveals, among other things, the weight of certain socio-cultural factors such as religious proscriptions (the role of the Reformation) or the negative influence of fairground hawkers whose use of the magic lantern caused it to be considered unworthy of adoption as a teaching aid.

The time lags observed in the use of audio-visual aids can be noted again in the use of educational games. Although such games have been known since ancient times, their large-scale introduction into school work only goes back, according to M.-M. Rabecq-Maillard, to the beginning of the present century[22]. Traditional games such as *le jeu de l'oie* (somewhat similar to

Snakes and Ladders) often borrow motifs from contemporary political or social events. Thus their history enables us to follow certain aspects of the evolution of society.

Among the traditional toys, the doll has become an object of attention on the part of some historians. Like the schoolbook, the doll can be considered from different angles. In this connection, M. Manson considers that 'to write the history of the doll is equivalent to working out a semiology of the toy as object in its relations with infantile play, with the adult imagination and with the overall socio-economic structure'[23]. For example, the relation between the adult imagination and the doll is interpreted on the basis on the ancient myth of Pygmalion. Among the sources explored in constructing this history are patents, the statutes of corporations of knick-knack and doll sellers, works of literature and folk tales.

The history of educational aids and objects now brings us to the behaviour of the teachers and pupils who use them.

The givers and receivers of education:
teacher training and women's education

Certain distinctions, well anchored in the education system, such as separation of the sexes or social discrimination, have led some historians to investigate the groups hitherto considered of lesser importance, for example women, children and adults of the lower classes, or the indigenous pupils of Third World countries during the colonial era.

In this connection, F. Mayeur has written two important works on the education of girls. One of them studies the daily regime of girls from comfortably off families in the nineteenth century with the object of 'finding out how women, as moulded by the customs and trends of a society, really were, without taking any account of edifying speeches'[24]. Thus the matter of education reveals itself as a social and political one: 'for women, can work be anything other than a sign of economic inferiority? Can it be a means of access to personal independence?' The author's second work deals with the drawing up and application of the Camille Sée Law (1880) which officially established secondary education for women[25]. Regarding this law, the author points out a number of contradictions with which any reform or innovation would find itself confronted. Thus, for example, while referring implicitly to the traditional social role of women, and while entrusting secondary teachers of girls with the task of producing wives and mothers rather than workers, the legislature nevertheless recruits female staff in order to carry out the task. It thus negates the initial conditions of its own project by creating a new career for women in the form of teaching. In addition, though designed for the education of adolescent girls from a well-to-do background, female secondary education gave young girls from poor families a means of access to the teaching profession, in other words to a modest but nevertheless independent position. In addition, the secondary education of women, with its republican origins, was organized in such a way as to be virtually identical to confessional education. In order to attract the middle classes, girls' *lycées* had to offer the same moral guarantees as the religious institutions. Thus it was indispensable for women teachers to be distinguished, well dressed, irreproachable in their conduct, in short, to be 'a kind of lay nun'.

Thus, while yielding to prejudice and conforming to the ideas of the time, women's secondary education immediately became a field for innovation and upheaval. In the long term, it was clearing the way for the feminization of the teaching profession and the evolution of the image of women in society.

The psychological and sociological analysis of the teaching profession, the circumstances in which it is recruited and trained, and the nature of its aspirations and ideology have been the object of various research projects.

For example, the perusal of 4,000 'instigated autobiographies' of primary school teachers during the *belle époque*, who began their careers between 1900 and 1914, has enabled J. Ozouf to demonstrate, among other things, how these teachers felt themselves to be entrusted with a political mission, i.e. to propagate the republican lay ideal. They felt themselves to be backed up in this course, even if they had to live through local unrest aroused by the institution of compulsory schooling, or by the conflicts between Church and State, which were sometimes quite dramatic[26].

These power contests reveal the difficulties encountered at the end of the eighteenth century by the Parisian parliamentarians in their efforts to establish, following the expulsion of the Jesuits (1762), a veritable national education system and a body of teachers recruited solely on the basis of their academic competence. In effect, the creation of the *agrégation* in the Paris Faculty of Arts (1766) excited lively opposition on the part of university personnel and members of religious congregations. Both considered that a competition based on examination did not make it possible to judge a candidate's talent and taste for the profession, and risked, moreover, opening the doors of the colleges to the enemies of religion[27].

One hundred years later, the creation of the *Ecole normale supérieure* at Saint-Cloud, intended to train lecturers for the primary school-teachers' training colleges, triggered a new power contest. 'Primary education teachers are willing,' wrote J.-N. Luc in this connection, 'to entrust the training of future teachers to the universities, but, in order to rest masters in their own house, they insist on its being organized outside the faculties . . . The problem raised at that time is still a topical one'[28].

From a comparative point of view, M. De Vroede presents the two models which emerged at the end of the eighteenth century and which, it would seem, gave rise to the structures of primary school-teacher training throughout Europe[29]. The first model, of which the Austrian *Normalschule* is typical, provides for courses of no more than a few weeks or months in a primary school chosen for the purpose. The second, represented by the Prussian *Lehrerseminar*, offers a course of theoretical and practical studies lasting three years, with residence and a school of practice. In the evolution of teacher training during the nineteenth century the author also observes similarities between Prussia and the United Kingdom. In both cases, the ambitious goals of the first half of the century were forced to give place, from 1850 on, to modest projects of strictly professional training. It remains to investigate the circumstances, whether internal or external to the education system, of this apparent step backwards.

The comparative history of education systems

From the standpoint of the history of ideas and doctrines, the history of education has no frontiers. The works of Plato, Erasmus, Comenius, Rousseau and Dewey are examined in all treatises on education. However, when the historian considers the working of the school system or the social aspects of education, he will tend to remain within a national or regional framework in order to satisfy certain methodological requirements[30]. A feature of recent years has nevertheless been a growing awareness of the existence of problem areas common to different countries belonging to a particular historical or geographical group, such as the Western countries or the Third World. Thus, W. Frijhoff compares the results of enquiries carried out respectively in France and Germany on the origins and careers of secondary school pupils during the second half of the nineteenth century. Whereas administration and the liberal professions exercised a great attraction on the young Germans, their opposite numbers in France were above all attracted to the land, the Stock Exchange and technology. But if we investigate their actual careers, we find these tendencies reversed. Whereas the French élite with its engineering qualifications went into government service, the German élite had more of a tendency to turn to industry[31].

A comparative study by A. Guillain investigates the similarities and differences between the educational psychology of J.F. Herbart, much applied in Germany at the end of the nineteenth century, and the natural education advocated by 'child study' in the United States. In both cases, one of the major political functions of the school was to preach and maintain national unity through moral, social and religious education. But whereas the disciples of Herbart tried to impose a single model to which everybody was supposed to conform, 'child study' respected the differences between individuals whose free and spontaneous interplay was supposed to ensure the emergence of a norm which would finally impose itself without any constraint[32].

Behind teaching methods and educational psychology, according to S.D. Ivie, one can discern the social myths affecting the structures, functions, content and methods of education. In the light of these myths – belief in the divinity of the emperor or in the superiority of the Aryan race – the author compares the educational experience of Japan and Germany in the course of the years preceding the Second World War[33]. In each of these countries, the myth fulfilled five functions: preservation of the sense of collective identity; solidarity; incitement to action; the legitimation of authority; and the inculcation of ideology. If we take the legitimation of authority, the relationship between the emperor and his subjects would have been understood in Japan as a logical extension of that between parents and children. In Germany, the myth of the master race served among other things to justify the creation of a new élite.

Comparative studies sometimes concern only one country, reporting on regional or local disparities in the percentage of the population attending school, success rates in examinations or the quantity of school equipment. Thus, in studying the evolution of attendance at kindergartens in Paris between 1945 and 1975, E. Plaisance shows that it was in the most bourgeois districts, where the proportion of professional people and senior civil servants was highest, that the rate of pre-school education increased the most[34].

The spread of comparative studies in the field of the history of education has led some research workers to sketch the profile of the qualifications of the authors of such studies. In the view of R. Koehl, the comparative researcher should be familiar with the history of education in both the societies under examination in order to compare data relating not only to education, but also to important aspects of economic, social or political life[35].

Whatever the goal and the terms of the comparison, the observation of similarities and differences must be completed by an analysis of the factors in play. This kind of analysis will be outlined in Part Two of the present work, in connection with regional disparities with regard to literacy.

In ending this brief survey of the most popular current themes among educational historians, the interest aroused by the subject of education in Third World countries during the colonial era should be emphasized.

The history of Third World countries

In the study of the past in Third World countries, some historians try to define the educative structures which existed prior to occupation by the colonial power[36]. More, however, are concerned with the colonial period itself, either comparing the situation in the colony with that in the colonizing country, or scrutinizing the functions fulfilled by the school system in the colonies.

In this connection, F. Colonna has examined official documents relating to the primary teachers' training college of Algiers in order to study the training and role of 'native' teachers. Referring to the theories of P. Bourdieu on the functions of the school, Colonna considers that this role consists of serving as cultural mediators between the colonial power and the mass of Algerians, to propagate the 'legitimate' culture as opposed to the 'barbarian' one, in other words to magnify the civilizing mission of France[37]. At the beginning of the twentieth century, there were two opposing models for the organization and content of teacher training. On the one hand, there was the segregationist doctrine, which consisted of designing a more elementary, more pragmatic training for indigenous student teachers than was given to their French opposite numbers, whether the latter were resident in the colony or in France. On the other hand, there was an assimilationist doctrine according to which the two groups should receive the same training. This second doctrine prevailed at the beginning of the 1920s on account of the evolution of the political and economic situation. However, it was not long before the logic of its own development caused the limitations and contradictions of the assimilation doctrine to appear. In effect, the colonial power judged it neither possible nor desirable for all Algerian children to go to school. The result was a current of educational demands forming part of the larger movement of opposition.

This boomerang effect is found in another form in the outcome of the educational work carried out in Zaire, formerly the Belgian Congo, by the Christian missionaries[38].

From the end of the nineteenth century on, these missions organized vocational education for young Congolese. In certain cases, on-the-job training in productive occupations such as agriculture and building was designed to achieve goals both practical and moral – 'The Gospel of Work'. In other cases, the chapel farms provided an initiation in traditional cultural behaviour. The most brilliant pupils received advanced religious training with a view to serving at mass, taking the chair at religious assemblies or teaching the catechism. The objectives of the vocational training of Congolese were defined in 1909 at the Catholic Congress of Belgium by a professor of the University of Louvain: 'It will not be necessary to aim too high and want to train perfect workers capable of competing with European workers.' In addition, the on-the-job training organized by the Jesuits in various trades such as carpentry, cooking and garment-making, was considered a suitable means of increasing the resources of a Company and thus of extending its proselytizing action.

While the missions succeeded in their project to train clerks and auxiliaries for the church, they did not succeed in holding on to the agricultural workers or artisans, who flocked in large numbers to the towns where they found work less on account of their technical competence than of their basic education and their habits of work. Thus, contrary to their expectations or their intentions, the missionaries provided the workforce that the colonial system required.

Whether proposed by the missionaries or by the State, the offer of education was far from being always welcomed by the native populations. In this connection, Y. Turin emphasizes the scale of the cultural resistance, particularly in the course of the first decades following the occupation of Algeria by France[39].

The cultural confrontations characteristic of the colonial period persisted in new forms after the Third World countries became independent. Torn between a need for cultural identity and an aspiration to modernity, these countries continued to experience in a sometimes dramatic way certain cultural legacies of colonization. This problem is examined by C. Fitouri from the point of view of the relationship between bilingualism and biculturalism[40]. More precisely, he attempts to find out the extent to which the introduction to a foreign culture (in this case Franco-occidental) and to a second language (French), plays a part in the success or failure of the present-day pupil in Tunisia. At the end of his empirical and reflective historical essay, Fitouri affirms the primacy of cultural and educational influences over linguistic ones.

The renewal of the historiography of the Third World is usually seen within the framework of an effort to attain or preserve a sense of identity on the part of the peoples concerned. In an essay on the socio-cultural characteristics of Algeria, A. Mazouni states that 'the only way . . . in which a really profound knowledge of the individuality of Algeria can be attained is by the writing of many monographs on the country and its population'[41]. He adds that 'the absence of prejudice in analysis does not exclude a deliberate commitment to progress'.

However, the question may be asked whether all the historians and would-be historians are always able to drawn the distinction between, on the one hand, the heuristic value which *may* be contained in a political or ideological commitment and, on the other, the explanatory or demonstrative quality which any truly scientific work *must* necessarily possess.

This difficult problem has already been evoked in relation to the functions of the school. We shall run into it again when we come to consider the methodological or technical orientations of educational historians.

NOTES AND REFERENCES

1. Veyne, P. *Comment on écrit l'histoire*. Paris, Seuil, 1971.
2. Brickman, W.W. Theoretical and critical perspectives on educational history. *Paedagogica historica* (Ghent, Belgium), no. 1, 1978, p. 42–83.
3. Mialaret, G.; Vial, J., eds. *Histoire mondiale de l'éducation*. Paris, Presses universitaires de France, 1981. 4 v.
4. *The international newsletter for the history of education*, published under the direction of Prof. M. Heinemann of the University of Hannover.

5. We take this opportunity of warmly thanking those colleagues who were kind enough to reply to the enquiry, viz.: Dr P.J. Cunningham (Oxford); Professor K. de Clerck (Ghent); Professor F.P. Hager (Zürich); Professor J. Herbst (University of Wisconsin); Professor J. Miaso (Warsaw); Dr. O. Vág (Budapest); and Z.A. Malkova (Academy of Pedagogical Sciences of the USSR).

6. Ivie, S.D. Myth and education. *Journal of thought* (Fayetteville, AR, University of Arkansas), vol. 6, no. 3, July 1971, p. 144–153.

7. Caplat, G.; Caspard, P. L'histoire de l'éducation à l'INRP. *Etapes de la recherche: bulletin d'information de l'Institut national de recherche pédagogique* (Paris), no. 4, novembre 1981, p. 1.

8. Caspard-Karydis, P., et al. *La presse d'éducation et d'enseignement, XVIIIᵉ siècle–1940.* Paris, INRP-CNRS, 1981.

9. Webster, C. Changing perspectives in the history of education. *Oxford review of education* (Oxford, United Kingdom), vol. 2, no. 3, 1976, p. 201–213.

10. Compère, Marie-Madeleine; Julia, D. Les collèges sous l'Ancien Régime: présentation d'un instrument du travail. *Histoire de l'éducation* (Paris, Institut national de recherche pédagogique), no. 13, décembre 1981, p. 1–27.

11. Frijhoff, W.; Julia, D. *Ecole et société dans la France d'Ancien Régime.* Paris, Colin, 1975.

12. Toulier, B. L'architecture scolaire aux XIXᵉ siècle: de l'usage de modèles pour l'édification des écoles primaires. *Histoire de l'éducation* (Paris, Institut national de recherche pédagogique), no. 17, décembre 1982, p. 1–29.

13. Julia, D. *Les trois couleurs du tableau noir. La Révolution.* Paris, Belin, 1981. 394 p.

14. Giolitto, P. *Histoire de l'enseignment primaire aux XIXᵉ siécle: l'organisation pédagogique.* Paris, Nathan, 1983. 288 p.

15. Contou, J. *Les punitions dans les lycées et collèges de l'instruction publique en France au XIXᵉ siécle (1814–1854).* Paris, Université de Paris V, 1980. 2 v. [Thèse]

16. Giolitto, P. *Op. cit.*

17. Ventre-Denis, M. Sciences sociales et université au XIXᵉ siècle. Une tentative d'enseignement de l'économie politique à Paris sous la Restauration. *Revue historique* (Paris), no. 520, 1976, p. 321–342.

18. Vial, J. Pour une histoire des objets pédagogiques. *Revue française de pédagogie* (Paris, Institut national de recherche et de documentation pédagogiques), no. 27, avril–mai–juin 1974, p. 43–46.

19. Choppin, A. L'histoire des manuels scolaires: une approche globale. *Histoire de l'éducation* (Paris, Institut national de recherche pédagogique), no. 9, décembre 1980, p. 1–25.

20. Perriault, J. *Mémoires de l'ombre et du son: une archéologie de l'audiovisuel.* Paris, Flammarion, 1981. 288 p.

21. Thollon-Pommerol, C. Pédagogie audio-visuelle: histoire et actualité. *Cahiers de la Section Sciences de l'éducation de l'Université de Genève* (Geneva), no. 35, 1983.

22. Rabecq-Maillard, Marie-Madeleine. *Histoire des jeux éducatifs.* Paris, Nathan, 1969, p. 64.

23. Manson, M. La poupée, objet de recherches pluridisciplinaires: bilan, méthodes et perspectives. *Histoire de l'éducation* (Paris, Institut national de recherche pédagogique), no. 18, avril 1983, p. 1–27.

24. Mayeur, Françoise. *L'éducation des filles en France au XIXᵉ siècle.* Paris, Hachette, 1979. 208 p.

25. Mayeur, Françoise. *L'enseignement secondaire des jeunes filles sous la Troisième République.* Paris, Presses de la Fondation nationale des sciences politiques, 1977. 488 p.

26. Ozouf, J. *Nous les maîtres d'école: autobiographie d'instituteurs de la Belle Epoque.* Paris, Gallimard, 1967.

27. Julia, D. La naissance du corps professoral. *Actes de la recherche en sciences sociales* (Paris, Maison des sciences de l'Homme), no. 39, 1981, p. 71–86.

28. Luc, J.-N. La formation des professeurs de maîtres d'école en France avant 1914: l'Ecole

34   *The history of education today*

normale supérieure de Saint-Cloud. *Revue française de pédagogie* (Paris, Institut national de recherche pédagogique), no. 51, avril–mai–juin 1980, p. 50–57.

29.   Vroede, M. De. La formation des maîtres en Europe jusqu'en 1914. *Histoire de l'éducation* (Paris, Institut national de recherche pédagogique), no. 6, avril 1980, p. 35–46.

30.   Frijhoff, W. Sur l'utilité d'une histoire comparée des systèmes éducatifs nationaux. *Histoire de l'éducation* (Paris, Institut national de recherche pédagogique), no. 13, décembre 1981, p. 30–44.

31.   Ibid.

32.   Guillain, A. L'éducation et le problème de l'unité nationale. Analyse comparée de deux exemples: l'Empire allemand et les Etats-Unis. 10 p. [Paper presented at the third Symposium of the International Association for the History of Education, Sèvres, 1981]

33.   Ivie, S.D. *Op. cit.* (See no. 6 above)

34.   Plaisance, E. Familles bourgeoises et scolarisation des jeunes enfants: la fréquentation des écoles maternelles publiques à Paris de 1945–1975. *Revue française de sociologie* (Paris, Centre national de la recherche scientifique), vol. 24, no. 1, janvier–mars 1983, p. 31–60.

35.   Koehl, R. Toward a comparative history of education. *Comparative education review* (Los Angeles, CA), vol. 18, no. 1, February 1974, p. 6–9.

36.   Emerit, M. L'état intellectuel et moral de l'Algérie en 1830. *Revue d'histoire moderne et contemporaine* (Paris, Société d'histoire moderne et contemporaine), vol. 1, 1954, p. 199–212.

37.   Colonna, Fanny. *Instituteurs algériens, 1883–1939.* Paris, Presses de la Fondation nationale des sciences politiques, 1975. 240 p.

38.   Yates, Barbara A. The triumph and failure of mission: vocational education in Zaire, 1879–1908. *Comparative education review* (Los Angeles, CA), vol. 20, no. 2, June 1976, p. 193–208.

39.   Turin, Y. *Affrontements culturels dans l'Algérie coloniale.* Paris, Maspéro, 1971.

40.   Fitouri, C. *Biculturalisme, bilinguisme et éducation.* Neuchâtel, Switzerland, Delachaux & Niestlé, 1983. 300 p.

41.   Mazouni, A. *Culture et enseignement en Algérie et au Maghreb.* Paris, Maspéro, 1969. 247 p.

CHAPTER III

Research orientations in the history of education

Like the interest aroused by history, the activity of the historian is historically determined. In effect, at a time when yesterday's triumphal version of school history is being called into question, writes M. Crubellier, historians 'are restricting the field of their enquiries, tending to abandon the broad synthesis and keeping more to the list of sources or the analysis of very precise problems which have hitherto been too much neglected'[1].

However, the reactions aroused by the teaching crisis, notably the feeling of not being able to control a complex situation, of not being able to grasp its factors and mechanisms, sometimes lead people to seek compensation in theorizing and in the working out of vast syntheses where the desire for internal coherence conceals or attenuates the need for external checking by recourse to sources or various kinds of testimonies.

This first contradiction is just one way, among others, of categorizing the activities of the educational historian.

Concerning histories of education

Other contradictions may be grouped under three headings, as follows:

The view of the relations between education and society. Certain opposing viewpoints are based on this factor. The controversies mentioned in the first chapter, which underlie the advent of the 'new history' or the revisionist trend, relate to the functions – integration or liberation – conferred on the school. In this respect the *projection* on the past of currently topical themes, such as the school's reproductive function or the deschooling of education, is the counterpart or complement of the process of *recovering* history with a view to supporting or justifying certain theories or actions. Thus, in French

schoolbooks of the early part of the Third Republic, the superstitions of the
Gauls are considered not as a phenomenon to be explained in the context of
its own time, but as the origin or model of obscure, archaic practices which
republican rationalism and the lay school wanted to eliminate[2]. In the
United States, the revisionists make use of a certain interpretation of the
negative role of the school in the nineteenth century to back up their theory
of the deschooling of society.

Outside the education system, the past is sometimes used in a selective or
tendentious way to influence present-day behaviour. Take the example of
the *metis* or half-breed mentality, a form of intelligence highly regarded in
the cultural universe of ancient Greece. Characterized among other things by a
tendency not to take up sharply defined positions, a certain shrewd carefulness,
dissimulation and resourcefulness, this mentality is nowadays sometimes
referred to as a source of irrational conduct whereas its analysis has called for
strictly rational procedures on the part of historians of psychology[3].

The importance of the rejection and recovery mechanisms can lead a historian
to slant his work towards some arbitrary interpretation, the internal coherence
of which will be ensured by his intentions or his ideology. It is of course often
difficult to reject such bias inasmuch as in history, as in other human sciences,
the illustration of a point of view is sometimes given as a proof.

We shall return to these methodological problems in Part Two where we shall
be less concerned with studying the functions and effects of public education
than with the conditions and contributing factors of the development of the
school. We shall return to them in Part Three, when we come to consider the
functions of history and, in particular, of the history of education.

The subdivision of the history of education. A second set of contradictions
arise from disagreement over this aspect. Each of the themes presented in the
last chapter, whether regarding the organization of the class, the recruitment
of teachers or the use of audio-visual aids, can be studied from either a long-
term or a short-term point of view.

Among the long-term phenomena we may note, for example, the study
and popularity of certain subjects, including technical ones; the cyclical return
of questions regarding the purpose of the school; or the secular superiority of
the north of France relative to the south with regard to the rate of literacy[4],
the dividing line running from Mont-Saint-Michel to Geneva. The long-term
point of view is also *de rigueur* when considering the history of education in
the context of social and cultural evolution. In this case, the historian is led
to play down the role of the school as an institution and to propose new
criteria for chronological subdivision. In Crubellier's view, the period of primacy of the immediate environment (family, parish, or village community)
gave way to a period of cultural domination by Church and State via the
school[5]. With regard to the family and changes of attitude to education, P.

Ariès and L. de Mause agree in situating the origins of modern conceptions of childhood in the sixteenth and seventeenth centuries, in conjunction with the development of the school system and the classification of pupils by age group. But whereas Ariès, a long-term historian, considers that this evolution takes place within a framework of broad slow cultural change, de Mause, on the basis of psychological history, attaches more importance to the direct influence of tensions between parents and children, emphasizing repressive practices and infanticide. In this connection, C. Webster writes that the public school in the United States was constructed on the basis of parental anxiety and of a fear of childhood; thus it appears as the result of an alliance between parents and teachers, and not as an institution at the service of childhood[6].

The points of view of Ariès and de Mause lend themselves to a discussion of the relative importance and organization of the factors of change in education. This discussion will be taken up in Part Two of the present study. Here we shall confine ourselves to emphasizing the limitations of a long-term approach to educational problems. More precisely, does the current situation of technical education as a kind of 'poor relation' stem simply from the effect of century-old prejudices? Can the failure of literacy campaigns and the difficulties of imposing universal education in Third World countries be imputed solely to the colonial heritage? According to M. Debeauvais, these problems 'are no longer concerned solely with the colonial heritage but also with the role of education systems in the reproduction of social and economic inequalities inside each country, and of international inequalities in the context of the division of labour between industrial countries and those of the Third World'[7]. This opinion restates the need for the educational historian to take note of present-day economic, social and political realities, and also to make the most of analysis of these realities.

Methodological aspects of historical research. A third series of contradictions is concerned above all with this aspect, although it is always difficult to decide on the relative importance of doctrinal factors on the one hand and an approach designed to reply to a question or to test a theory on the other.

In this respect, we have to draw a distinction between a *unidimensional* history of education and a *multidimensional* history associating the educational field with others such as economics, politics or religion. The concept of 'total history', linked, as we have seen, to the emergence of the 'new history', is an expression of the multidimensional mode. The same is true of the analysis of relations between science and ideology, with respect to the definition of complex notions such as that of aptitude[8].

Another couple of opposites are *descriptive* (or what one might describe as 'free') *history* and *functional history*, which highlights events and conflicts which might, in the long or the short term, influence educational situations.

According to L. Goldmann, the choice of this second approach makes it necessary to take into account 'human action anywhere and at any time, in so far as it has or has had some importance for or an effect on the existence and structure of some group of human beings and thus, implicitly, of the present or future human community'[9]. For example, in France, both at the time and afterwards, the war of 1870 and the Paris Commune aroused social and political reactions tending to a redefinition of the functions and a change in the methods and content of primary and adult education[10].

From an apparently more technical point of view, it is possible to distinguish, on the one hand, a tendency to put together homogeneous series (such as costs, numbers, premises, content of programmes, etc.) with a view to quantitative and long-term analysis; and, on the other, a desire to go more deeply into the study of a single phenomenon – for example, a vote or the application of a reform – by collecting heterogeneous material (such as data on social and political conditions and legal measures, or the reactions of educationists, pupils and public opinion, etc.). In the first case, writes F. Furet, 'the historical fact is built up through a time series of homogeneous and comparable units. This "serial" approach substitutes a regular distribution of data selected as a function of their comparability for the ungraspable event of the positivist approach. The event becomes a phenomenon chosen and perhaps constructed as a function of its repetitive nature'[11].

Certain documentary sources, such as schoolbooks or educational reviews, meet the requirements of 'serial' history quite easily. Other types of material, however, may lend themselves to a long-term and quantitative approach. Thus, analysis of the content of prize-giving speeches in French secondary schools between 1860 and 1965 has enabled V. Isambert-Jamati to study variations in educational goals as between one decade and another or one group of educationists and another. To a larger extent, this variation is ascribable to broad ideological trends reflecting both the state of social relations and the impact of certain political events. Thus, whereas the appreciation of supreme values such as the beautiful, the good or the true are the dominant themes of such speeches during the last ten years of the Second Empire, acquisition of the skills necessary for success took its place during the early years of the Third Republic, a period marked, among other things, by the defeat of 1870, the lay movement and colonial expansion[12].

What are the conditions and meaning of the development of quantitative techniques in the history of education? According to H.G. Graff, it can be accounted for by two types of factor.

In the first place, the partial taking over of education by social history has led research workers to take an interest in new subjects such as the family and demographic evolution, and to ask themselves questions in such new areas as the consequences of education for the individual and for society. Within this new framework, the educational historian cannot escape the need to have recourse to the quantification of data and the statistical treatment of results.

The second type of factor arises from the affirmation of the revisionist movement. In effect, those who belong to it need to make use of numerical data on social and geographical mobility, or on the distribution of health or income, in order to refute traditional doctrines concerning the functions of the school. Whatever the relative importance of these two types of factor, Graff refuses to reduce the quantitative approach to a simple technical problem. In his view, the approach is both conceptual and methodological, implying not only the search for new data but also the formulation of original questions and theories regarding the relations between social change and changes in the education system.

This conceptual and methodological evolution crops up again in the transition from narrative logic, in which what has occurred before explains what occurs afterwards, to the logic of social science, characterized by the urge to describe behaviour objectively and to determine its circumstances. In this connection, Furet[13] considers that period history, by which he means a chronological narrative aiming to reconstitute what has happened, is giving place to the history of phenomena, or the analytical study of a single theme over periods of time considered to be heterogeneous.

Nevertheless, many historians agree with Veyne that 'once they emerge from their documents and proceed to their synthesis, . . . they narrate real events in which men are the protagonists' and that 'history is a novel of real life'[14].

If history is a novel based on real life, it remains to determine what distinguishes it from one which is not. Perhaps this is the place to recall the possibility of a history 'oriented to the formulation and the re-formulation of problems, and to a clearer distinction between interpretation and what is based on research', in short of a history able to unmask both clever rationalizations (e.g. 'what happened was the only thing that could have happened') and a spontaneous acceptance of narrative logic[15].

Is it possible to assert, like L. Stone, that the survival or revival of narrative history is due to the decline of certain deterministic approaches, to the failure of attempts to reply to the big questions? According to E. Hobsbawm, 'it is a case less of substitution than of complementarity between, on the one hand, the analysis of socio-economic structures and movements, and, on the other, the history of human beings and their states of mind'. In short, 'there is nothing new in the decision to look at the world through a microscope rather than through a telescope'[16].

In any event, the contrast coupling of thematic history and narrative history relates to another such pair of opposing doctrines, i.e. laying the emphasis on circumstances or laying the emphasis on human beings.

The latter school of thought is illustrated by the success of a history of outlooks. Founded some fifty years ago by Bloch and Febvre, and long confined to the Middle Ages and the Renaissance, the history of ideas nowadays extends towards the modern and contemporary periods. According to Agulhon, this extension is due to the joint progress of ethnology, historical demography and, in particular, social history. In this respect, the attention given to the collective protagonists of historical movements has led to an awareness of their particular ways of thinking or acting and to a rejection of anachronism in the interpretation of their motives, their perceptions and their feelings. 'Although revolutionaries,' states Agulhon, "may well have in mind the doctrines and programmes of the revolution ... their behaviour is also determined by more spontaneous, non-intellectual factors, and that is why historians have deliberately adopted the concept of outlook (*mentalités*)'[17]. According to Michel Vovelle, the notion of outlook refers, relative to that of ideology, to a longer period of time, to memory, to 'the inertia of mental structures'. For many specialists, the 'climb from the basement to the attic', or in other words from social history to the history of outlooks, appears as an enlargement of the field of research. They conceive the history of outlooks as 'the study of mediations and of the dialectic relationship between the objective conditions of human life and the way it is told or even experienced'[18].

This focus on outlook has brought about certain changes in historical practice. In particular, it has given rise to a systematic use of indirect testimony. Thus, in portraying the characteristics of popular culture in the sixteenth century, in order better to grasp the views of the world which in those days were transmitted orally, R. Muchembled calls upon 'the forces of repression to relate the history of what they were trying to repress'[19]. In the same way, in drawing up his *Dictionnaire biographique du mouvement ouvrier français*, J. Maitron draws, among other sources, on the *Gazette des tribunaux* in order to portray the life and action of obscure militants[20].

At the same time as it enlarges the field of historical enquiry and the techniques of investigation, the flowering of the history of outlooks may correspond to a need for compensation *vis-à-vis* the ruptures and uprootings caused by the rapid changes in economic, social and cultural life. Its object is indeed to recreate for us the emotions, beliefs and representations of our ancestors. However, according to Furet, 'it is not so much concerned with explaining what is strange as with finding the familiar behind the illusion of strangeness. Thus it contains the seeds of a temptation to picturesqueness, which constitutes its link with the public at large'[21]. Furthermore, if applied to the study of colonized peoples, the notion of outlook sends us back to a static psychology recalling summary judgements about the supposedly permanent characteristics (for example impulsiveness, vindictiveness, fatalism and so on) of the 'natives'[22].

Thus it would be better to replace it by the more dynamic notion of personality building itself in action. In this connection, we may regret that as a rule historians pay little attention to the orientations of psychological history. The founders of this discipline considered that intellectual and affective functions are 'by their nature subject to change, imperfect and imperfectible' and asked questions about the origin of certain forms of conduct such as the memorization of a story or the representation of the notion of work[23].

Consider, for example, the representation of the notion of work. In ancient Greece, farm work was not perceived as a job but rather as an attempt to obtain divine blessings. The exercise of a craft was seen as an extention of the natural qualities of the craftsman and not as part of a division of labour which would optimize productivity. Closer to our own time, in the nineteenth century, the function of labour grows blurred, in the writings of the followers of Saint-Simon, behind that of an industrial order of society, the noun *industriel* (industrialist) applies at that time equally well to the workman, the engineer or the owner. If we turn to the school of the disciples of Fourier, we find the idea of labour eclipsed behind the mechanism of passion. In other words, far from being the motive force, work is itself motivated by the passions[24].

The evolution of the relations between the various branches of historical research affects the status and functions of history. Thus, by concentrating on the study of particular problems such as the modalities of school streaming or of the teaching of a subject, rather than on national systems of education, history becomes an instrument of communication between the specialists of different countries and accordingly a better instrument of comparative research. At the same time, in so far as they are increasingly aware of the context or the spirit of a period, historians cease to sit in judgement on the people or actions of the past.

However, in rejecting any linear image of evolution, does not the 'new history' call into question the very concept which makes the time scale the basis of the evaluation of progress? Does it not cast doubt on the sense of the history of education? Moreover, does not the devaluation of national themes bring with it the danger of depriving historians – and their readers – of an important source of motivation?

These complex problems will be taken up and discussed again in Part Three and in the conclusion of the present book, with respect to the functions of history and the notion of progress.

Educational historians

The alternative viewpoints proposed in this chapter may cast some light on the orientations of educational historians. Naturally, these distinctions are of a schematic kind, and the same historian may from time to time apply several approaches, no doubt different but often complementary, and in any case not exclusive. Nevertheless, the tendency to prefer one approach, one kind of subject matter, or one particular way of managing and interpreting data allows us to sketch out the outline of certain categories of social historian without, however, falling into the excess of a too rigid typology.

First of all comes the *scholar* whose basic activity is research into new sources of documentation and whose ambition is either to provide working instruments or collections of texts for the use of the other historians, or to paint a picture as complete and precise as possible of some doctrine, work, institution or educational practice. The work of collecting and organizing material may give rise to different strategies. E. Le Roy Ladurie distinguishes two kinds of historian, 'the truffle seeker and the parachutist. The truffle seeker finds a treasure, a rare document, rich with promise. The parachutist ... rakes over a broad terrain, thanks notably to quantative methods.' The author adds that the ideal would be to be both at the same time.

Often, the historian is concerned not only with reconstructing what really happened but also with recreating the way in which what happened was seen and felt by people at the time. In this case he becomes a *historian of outlook*.

Let us take the example of infant care and, in particular, wet nursing. It was a response to concerns which have largely disappeared. An external sign of social rank, its object was not only to enable women in high society to fulfil their worldly obligations. It was also linked to the demographic situation at the time and to a certain view of biological mechanisms. In effect, in view of the very high rate of infant mortality, one did not become really attached to a child until it had reached the age where one might be reasonably sure of its survival. Moreover, because of the idea which people had of the interactions between the circulation of the blood (stimulated by sexual relations) and the production of milk (effected by these same relations), it was considered desirable during the period of breast-feeding to obviate all risk of the mixing of these two liquids, and to prescribe an abstinence with which the wet-nurses could, naturally, come to terms.[25]

Sometimes called upon to *synthesize*, the historian bases his analysis on the result of works of scholarship in painting broad canvases, whether synchronic or diachronic, of some educational institution and, in certain cases, outlines the laws underlying the trends. In the history of educational institutions, the rivalry between what Durkheim calls the formal and the realist trends stems from this approach. These laws will be discussed in Part Two.

More remote from works of scholarship, the *philosophical historian* analyses the works of the major educational writers in order to sketch the evolution of the goals of education, to follow the changes which have occurred in attitudes to children, or to study the heritage of Plato or Rousseau.

Proclaiming their allegiance to one school or another of *contemporary sociology*, some historians are occupied with analysing the workings of a particular sector of the education system, for example recruitment, curricula or the subsequent careers of pupils. Expressed in terms of the functions fulfilled by the school, their conclusions served to feed the controversies already mentioned above regarding the flowering of the 'new history' and the revisionist movement.

It happens that the sociological historian may also be a *statistician* or an *information specialist* interested in the quantitative analysis of temporal series of homogeneous units such as school numbers, the level of education among soldiers, or the number of adult education courses. This kind of activity will be discussed in Part Two in connection with work on literacy and the demand for education.

This rapid review of the activities of historians does not claim to be exhaustive. Nevertheless, it gives a sufficiently good picture of the diversity to make one wonder about the soundness of any project of selection and training common to all educational historians.

Does not each field and each approach impose its own methodological requirements? In attempting to define these requirements, in connection with the history of primary education in the nineteenth century, P. Caspard and J.N. Luc warn the research worker against 'the privileged rank wrongly accorded to the interpretation of official texts' and against 'broad generalizations', suggesting instead, on the one hand, that priority be given to a micro-historical approach to the workings of the education system and, on the other, that the necessary classifications of students should be made according to sex, socio-economic category or habitation[26].

Quite apart from methodological recommendations, Brickman sets out what he considers to be the desirable qualifications for historians in general[27]:

— a liberal education including literature, aesthetics, philosophy, the psychology of education, mathematics, etc.;
— a good knowledge of world history from ancient times down to the present day;
— an extensive knowledge of the history of education with respect to ideas, institutions, individuals, practices and results;
— a profound knowledge, on the basis of original sources, of at least one sector of the history of education;
— a mastery of historical research methods;
— a knowledge of the history of historiography; and
— the ability to read easily the languages used in the writing of history.

To this already substantial list of qualifications should be added the knowledge and capacity needed to carry on a dialogue implied by the strengthening of links between the history of education and other human sciences.

NOTES AND REFERENCES

1. Crubellier, M. L'histoire en crise d'une école en crise. *Histoire de l'éducation* (Paris, Institut national de recherche pédagogique), no. 18, avril 1983, p. 29.
2. Maingueneau, D. *Les livres d'écoles de la République (1870–1914): discours et idéologie.* Paris, Le Sycomore, 1979. 344 p.
3. Detienne, M.; Vernant, J.-P. *Les ruses de l'intelligence: la métis des Grecs.* Paris, Flammarion, 1978.
4. Rémond, R. Préface. *In:* Parias, L.-H., ed. *Histoire générale de l'enseignement et de l'éducation en France.* Paris, Nouvelle Librairie de France, 1981, t. 1, p. 30.
5. Crubellier, M. *L'enfance et la jeunesse dans la société française (1800–1950).* Paris, Colin, 1979.

6.   Webster, C. Changing perspectives in the history of education. *Oxford review of education* (Oxford, United Kingdom), vol. 2, no. 3, 1976, p. 210.
7.   Debeauvais, M. Education and a New International Economic Order. *Prospects* (Paris, Unesco), vol. XII, no. 2, 1982, p. 139.
8.   Léon, A. *Introduction à l'histoire des faits éducatifs.* Paris, Presses universitaires de France, 1980. 248 p.
9.   Goldmann, L. *Sciences humaines et philosophie.* Paris, Presses universitaires de France, 1952.
10. Léon, A. *Histoire de l'éducation populaire en France.* Paris, Nathan, 1983.
11. Furet, F. Le quantitatif en histoire. *In:* Le Goff, J.; Nora, P. *Faire l'histoire.* Paris, Gallimard, 1974.
12. Isambert-Jamati, V. *Crises de la société, crises de l'enseignement.* Paris, Presses universitaires de France, 1970. 400 p.
13. Furet, F. *L'atelier de l'histoire.* Paris, Flammarion, 1982. 320 p.
14. Veyne, P. *Comment on écrit l'histoire.* Paris, Seuil, 1971.
15. Furet, F. *Op. cit.*
16. Hobsbawm, E. Retour ou récit? Réponse à Lawrence Stone. *Le Débat* (Paris), no. 23, p. 153–160.
17. Agulhon, M. Histoire des mentalités. *In:* Comité français des sciences historiques. *La recherche historique en France depuis 1965.* Paris, Editions du Centre national de la recherche scientifique, 1980.
18. Vovelle, M. *Idéologies et mentalités.* Paris, Maspéro, 1982. 264 p.
19. Muchembled, R. *Culture populaire et culture des élites dans la France moderne, (XVᵉ–XVIIIᵉ siècle).* Paris, Flammarion, 1978. 400 p.
20. Maitron, J. *Dictionnaire biographique du mouvement ouvrier français.* Paris, Les Editions ouvrières, 1964.
21. Furet, F. *Op. cit.*
22. Lucas, P. *Problèmes de la transition au socialisme: le transformisme algérien.* Paris, Anthropos, 1979. 392 p.
23. Meyerson, I. *Les fonctions psychologiques et les œuvres.* Paris, Vrin, 1948. 224 p.
24. Meyerson, I.; Vernant, J.-P. et al. Le travail, fonction psychologique. *Journal de psychologie* (Paris), no. 1, 1955. [numéro spécial]
25. Peeters, H.F.M. L'enfant et l'adolescent étudiés dans une perspective historique. *Paedagogica historica* (Ghent, Belgium), vol. VIII, no. 2, 1968, p. 449–450.
26. Caspard, P.; Luc, J.N. Questions sur l'enseignement primaire au XIXᵉ siècle. *Histoire de l'éducation* (Paris, Institut national de recherche pédagogique), no. 6, avril 1980, p. 55–56.
27. Brickman, W.W. Theoretical and critical perspectives on educational history. *Paedagogica historica* (Ghent, Belgium), vol. XVIII, no. 1, 1978, p. 42–83.

CHAPTER IV

The history of education
in the context of the humanities

The historical study of an educational problem appears to confirm the words
of F. Braudel: 'History lends itself to dialogue. It has little structure of its
own, and is open to neighbouring sciences ... It is the most literary and
readable of human sciences, the most open to the public at large'[1]. No
doubt this point of view needs some toning down, particularly when quantitative historical research is taken into account. Moreover, even if technical
obstacles are left aside, can one say that the dialogue between historians
and the practitioners of other human sciences is always easy or even possible?

Should the notion of interdisciplinarity here raised be considered as a mere
product of wishful thinking, as the object of fruitless projects, or as the expression of useful and effective interaction?

Difficulties in the meeting of disciplines

It seems difficult to envisage the relations between the history of education and other human sciences from a global point of view. In effect, such
relations spring from different elements and thus raise a number of questions:
— What is the place of the history of education among other educational
   sciences such as educational psychology or sociology?
— What is the position of educational history *vis-à-vis* the other branches
   of history, notably in relation to social and cultural history?
— What could be the nature of the relations between the history of education and other human sciences sometimes called general or fundamental,
   such as psychology, sociology and demography?
Indeed, can it not be said that the same kind of problem arises in connection

with relations between movements or special fields within a single discipline, in this case the history of education?

For the moment, let us confine ourselves to this last question. The rapid growth of knowledge and the diversification of approaches and techniques lead some specialists to think that the gap between the different branches of a single discipline, or between research and application of the same discipline, can only continue to grow, thus rendering communication more and more difficult between persons whose collaboration would appear indispensable to the development of that particular field.

In psychology, for example, M. Reuchlin draws a distinction between those who accept and those who refuse the fundamental role of science, i.e. the explicit, public and verifiable nature of all proceedings and statements, or, to put it the other way, between those who accept and those who refuse a contamination of the scientific process by ideology. More precisely, 'it is because it wishes to be verifiable that scientific psychology imposes a technicality and constraints which might seem unacceptable to some, and that it must accept limited objectives; but it is precisely to the extent that it is verifiable that it possesses characteristics intrinsic to development. By the same token, it is because it ignores or postpones the exigencies of verification that clinical psychology enjoys a certain kind of success, but is also unable to know if and when progress is achieved'[2].

It would be possible to extend these remarks to other humanities and, for example, to draw a distinction between an essentially interpretative and sometimes dogmatic type of history, on the one hand, and, on the other, an approach to the subject whereby the historian attaches much value to documentary research, to explaining his processes and to placing his results in context.

Thus, as we have already had occasion to emphasize in the preceding chapter, there exist several schools of the history of education in the same way as there exist several schools of educational psychology or sociology.

This being so, one may wonder whether the respective contributions to any interdisciplinary relationship should not be quite widely differentiated. Thus, for example, one might study the relation between the demand for training as a contribution of educational history and the situation of the labour movement as a contribution of social history.

However, still other difficulties arise. These spring from the usual way of classifying disciplines, which tends to establish relations of dependence between them or which subordinates the part to the whole. Thus, in a work entitled *La recherche historique en France depuis 1965*[3], the history of education is incorporated in a section entitled 'Histoire culturelle et histoire de l'art'.

Other difficulties stem from the mobility or the disappearance of frontiers between disciplines. The historian P. Ariès writes in this connection:

It is a strange thing that whereas historians are tempted by synchronization, the human sciences often rebel against it, seeking a long-term point of view. This is why the gaps between history and the other human sciences are tending to narrow; an event more recent than one might imagine following fifty years of lip-service to interdisciplinarity, during which time it has never really been implemented[4].

The sociologist G. Vincent appears to agree with this opinion, defining the process of socialization in the following terms:

To speak of a socialization process, in the sense that one speaks of a production process, is not to designate a series of proceedings or agents such as the family, the school or the media, nor is it to describe the operation which culturalists have defined as the absorption of group values by individuals. It is rather to try to find out by what means a society creates and constantly recreates itself . . . it is rather to evoke contradictions, ambiguities, violence and resistance[5].

In the light of these two series of observations, is it right to speak of inter-disciplinary collaboration, or of a process of conversion, or even of contamination? Should one not rather emphasize the trend for history to become 'total' and even to set itself up as an 'overall human science'? Indeed, is interdisciplinarity conceivable at all if one has not first of all defined the field of each discipline, while nevertheless leaving room for the inevitable overlapping zones?

However that may be, the totalizing character of the 'new history' cannot help but give rise to fashions and to affect the behaviour of specialists. For an educational historian, not to draw attention to his involvement with social history or the history of outlooks is to run the risk of seeing himself classified for good among the latter-day positivists or, at least, among those who have ceased to be 'with it'. According to G. Bois:

What had been essentially a fruitful renewal of historical methodology was quickly changed by fashion following its first successes. Here was the 'new history' launched like a brand of detergent! Even if one remains attached to a narrative, unilinear and narrowly event-linked type of history, one will henceforth have to proclaim one's allegiance to the 'new school' in order to make the product easier to sell. Better still, we shall soon see the most empirical historians becoming enthusiastic promoters of statistical refinement. Thus, the introduction of simple techniques takes over from the working out of conceptual tools, and positivism finds a way to survive by dressing up in new clothes[6].

By way of complement to Bois's pertinent remarks, let us just add that many research workers did not wait for the exhortations of the 'new' historians in order to study such subjects as the social origin of pupils or the daily routine in the schools of bygone ages.

Sometimes, in the course of preparing a report or carrying out research, a particular research worker may become aware of relations between his own and some neighbouring or complementary speciality. This might for example be the case of a psychologist or sociologist who, upon the altar of academic requirements, introduced a historical dimension into the study of some basically psychological or sociological problem. In this connection, an analysis

analysis of theses reveals a frequent tendency to use the most questionable procedures and results of historiography. Over and above the inevitable errors, anachronisms or clichés, one can often observe an absence of any reference to the context, or an obsession with signing a precise date to the origin of an idea or an institution.

When the context is mentioned, it is often in the manner of a stylistic exercise. An author may speak vaguely of economic, social or cultural factors. In other cases, an impression of greater precision is given by stressing the importance of some factor such as the emergence of new social classes, an economic crisis or a demographic upsurge. But unless the relations between these factors and educational reality are gone into more deeply, the author does not succeed in going beyond a certain historical or sociological formalism.

Analysis of the troubled interface between disciplines cannot, however, mask the existence of reciprocal influences nor the prospect of mutual enrichment or the synergic deepening of knowledge.

Mutual enrichment

We have had several occasions to emphasize the importance of the role of sociology in enlarging the field and renewing the subject-matter of the history of education. In referring to this role with respect to the historical study of literacy, H.J. Graff considers that the progress achieved in this field is due less to educational historians than to the work of specialists in social mobility and demography[7]. This remark indirectly raises the question of the legitimacy of educational science.

Some authors consider that the influence of demography on history is greater than that of sociology[8]. Based as it is on parish registers, tax returns and other such records, demography brings fresh life to social history and the study of outlooks. As J. Dupâquier points out, 'instead of tackling the great problems of history – which are not always the real ones – with ridiculously inadequate measuring instruments, the sole ultimate use of which is to cover up the guesses and prejudices of authors, this approach brings down the level of observation to that of individuals and families'[9]. Thus, contrary to the stated opinions of certain historians based on the testimony of theologians or moralists, the population of France under the *ancien régime* appears to have respected the Commandments. Indeed, the proportion of extramarital births, nowadays 26 per cent, varied between 4 and 16 per cent before 1750.

Whatever the contributions of different social sciences to historical research, according to F. Furet, 'the act of learning to know the past cannot be separated from that of understanding the world in which we live'[10]. However, rooted as it is in the present, the historian's curiosity sometimes arouses phenomena of projection and recovery that American authors call 'presentism'.

By the same token, an understanding of history can affect research on present-day society and the individuals who make it up. Nor is this influence confined to finding historical explanations for contemporary problems. In effect, sooner or later, experts in all disciplines feel a need to go back to their sources and the process of their development in order to go more deeply into certain epistemological problems. For example, inasmuch as modern experimental pedagogy borrows the essence of its concepts and techniques from scientific psychology, one might be tempted to think that the latter is an older science than the former. This over-simplication is, however, called into question by the historical approach. In fact, experimental pedagogy has to a large extent developed independently or, more precisely, according to a process based both on purely educational needs and on models which existed well before the end of the nineteenth century[11]. Thus, the doctor and educator Jean Itard carried out a veritable educational experiment with a view to developing and controlling the capacities of the 'child savage' who had been entrusted to him.

Ignorance of historical aspects of behaviour can paralyse psychological research, as has been shown by P. Malrieu in his studies on relations between historical and genetic psychology. The latter has had to rid itself of the notion of immutable functions, essential to human nature. Thus, the disciples of Piaget admit 'the essential universality of basic cognitive structures' even if, from one country to another, cultural conditions impose differences in the rate and style of the construction of behaviour. For their part, psycholinguistic disciples of Chomsky emphasize the existence of 'fundamental structures' or 'universals'. Experimental psychologists, on the other hand, tend rather to study the relations between two functions (for example, memory and intelligence) than their 'interconstruction'. To sum up, in the view of Malrieu, genetic psychology must take the construction of behaviour as its object. This construction takes place via the child's various encounters with history. In effect, the psychological functions develop through the perception of manipulation of works, objects or instruments which are themselves historical products. Moreover, the adult with which the child identifies conveys modes of behaviour which are also products of history[12].

The problem of time is another meeting-place between historians and psychologists. According to the orientation of their research, they are both interested in experienced, perceived time (where there is an attitude, a feeling of duration and succession); or in the operative, measurable time of the collective consciousness; or in the conceived notional idea of time (notably with the respect to historical times) of the reflective consciousness. For example, attitudes to the passing of time underwent profound changes at the end of the Middle Ages. As J. Le Goff puts it, there was a transition at that time from 'church time' to 'merchant time'. Theological time, dominated by God, punctuated only by the rites of the church, gradually yielded to time as 'managed' by the merchant. In effect, the latter based his activity on temporal computations such as stocking with a view to subsequent shortages, buying and selling at the right moments, or the charging of interest which made it possible to realize a profit over a period of time[13]. Psychologists and historians study not only attitudes to time, but also the means adopted by people in order to evaluate it, defeat it or escape from it, by reference either to eternal principles or to tradition. The genetic psychologist takes a particular interest in the stages by which the child masters the idea of time, thus contributing to the educational psychology of history.

Quite apart from this exploration of the same subjects, historians and psychologists can also follow similar or converging lines in their own mono-disciplinary research. Thus, like certain historians, M. Richelle stresses, in a collective work entitled *Psychologie de demain*, the need to concentrate on the problems in hand rather than on the methods of explanation, or in other words to see science 'not as a set of certainties, but as a manner of asking questions'[14]. In the same work, with respect to the utilization of research results, P. Oleron proposes the establishment of psychology for everybody which would also be the psychology of everybody 'in so far as it would take into account the problems of daily life'[15].

By according priority to the problems and stressing the need to approach the same question on the basis of practical situations and from different points of view, it would be possible to arrive at a better definition of the place of the history of education among human sciences. It would also be possible to advance the study of interdisciplinarity among educational sciences.

Persistent differences

In this connection, it would be pointless to underestimate the differences separating history from psychology or other humanities. These differences relate to the possibilities of scientific rigour which each discipline offers.

According to G. Granger, history is 'a clinic without practice' and the historian 'a speculative clinician'[16]. These laconic definitions would appear to express a double impossibility: on the one hand, that of conceiving a technique of action on the basis of examples taken from the past; and on the other, that of affecting the object of study in order to know it better.

We shall be going more deeply into the first aspect of Granger's reflections in Part Three, dealing with the functions of history. As regards the speculative activity of the historian, it is a truism to state that he is unable to carry out any real experimentation, or in other words to reproduce the phenomenon under study after having determined the conditions of its appearance. Nevertheless, this impossibility cannot negate the requirement, common to the human sciences as a whole, to submit any proposition, hypothesis or opinion to checking against the facts. Naturally, whether we are talking about history or psychology, when a situation had been sufficiently well analysed to justify the formulation of an exact question, such a question will naturally call for a precise answer, perhaps with some indication as to probability or some discussion of the possibilities of generalization. To be more explicit, let us consider the function of the school. The general question of whether the school has in the past mirrored the social strata or whether in the long run it produced conditions such as to call those strata into question can only give rise to an ambiguous answer in so far as the two functions have always existed side by side, as can be shown by many examples. On the other hand, precise questions such as what was the origin of pupils in colleges under the *ancien régime*, or what professions were followed by young men from different social categories, can be answered precisely with respect to the sample of schools under consideration[17].

These comments on the degree to which various human sciences or approaches can be considered genuinely scientific do not in any way exhaust the subject of interdisciplinarity. There remain other questions to be gone into more deeply, such as that of the training and specialization (single or multiple) of the research worker, or that of the transfer of knowledge and attitudes when a specialist changes 'workshop' or discipline, whether temporarily or permanently. It also remains to envisage the conditions for the constitution of genuine multidisciplinary teams and their chances of success or survival in a scientific universe dominated by increasing specialization, compartmentalization, competition and conflicts between competing groups.

It sometimes happens that such disputes arise out of conflicting conceptions about change in education.

NOTES AND REFERENCES

1. Braudel, F. Universalité et diversité des sciences de l'homme. *Revue de l'enseignement supérieur* (Paris), no. 1, 1960, p. 17–22.
2. Reuchlin, M. Croisées de chemins. *In:* Fraisse, P., ed. *Psychologie de demain.* Paris, Presses universitaires de France, 1982.
3. Comité français des sciences historiques. *La recherche historique en France depuis 1965.* Paris, Eds. du Centre nationale de la recherche scientifique, 1980. 154 p.
4. Ariès, P. L'histoire des mentalités. *In:* Le Goff, J., ed. *La nouvelle histoire.* Paris, Retz, 1978, p. 411.
5. Vincent, G. Le groupe de recherches sur le procès de socialisation. *Histoire de l'éducation* (Paris, Institut national de recherche pédagogique), no. 18, avril 1983, p. 97.
6. Bois, G. Marxisme et histoire nouvelle. *In:* Le Goff, J., ed. *La nouvelle histoire.* Paris, Retz, 1978, p. 378.

7. Graff, H.J. 'The new math' quantification, the 'new' history and the history of education. *Urban education* (Beverley Hills, CA), vol. 11, 1977, no. 4, p. 403–440.
8. Furet, F. *L'atelier de l'histoire.* Paris, Flammarion, 1982.
9. Dupâquier, J. Histoire et démographie. *Population* (Paris, Institut national d'études démographiques), 1977, numéro spécial, p. 299–318.
10. Furet, F. *Op. cit.*
11. Léon, A. *Introduction à l'histoire des faits éducatifs.* Paris, Presses universitaires de France, 1980. 248 p.
12. Malrieu, P. Psychologies génétiques et psychologie historique. *Journal de psychologie normale et pathologique* (Paris), no. 3, juillet–septembre 1978, p. 261–277.
13. Le Goff, J. Au Moyen Age: temps de l'Eglise et temps des marchands. *Annales* (Paris), 1960, p. 417–433.
14. Richelle, M. Craintes et espérance pour la psychologie de l'an 2000. *In:* Fraisse, P., ed. *Psychologie de demain.* Paris, Presses universitaires de France, 1982.
15. Oleron, P. Demain, une psychologie pour tous? *In:* Fraisse, P., ed. *Psychologie de demain.* Paris, Presses universitaires de France, 1982.
16. Granger, G. *Pensée formelle et sciences de l'homme.* Paris, Aubier-Montaigne, 1968. 228 p.
17. Frijhoff, M.; Julia, D. *Ecole et société dans la France d'Ancien Régime.* Paris, Colin, 1975.

PART TWO

Change in education: concepts, factors, mechanisms

CHAPTER V

Concepts of change in education

After the completion of the manuscript of the present work, two important books on the theories of change were published: *Le changement social: tendances et paradigmes* by M. Forsé and H. Mendras (Paris, Colin, 1983) and *La place du désordre: critiques des théories du changement social* by R. Boudon (Paris, Presses universitaires de France, 1984). In the first work, the authors attempt to build models suitable to explain various categories of social transformation, on the basis of a study of actual cases. By a treatment at once more epistemological and more methodological, Boudon's book analyses the reasons for the failure of general conceptions of social change and sets out the necessary conditions for establishing valid theories. Thus the author expresses an attitude which is critical and relativist, but not sceptical, as regards the current debates on change.

The study of the relations between changes in education and in social life covers different levels of reflective or philosophical analysis and of empirical research.
In the most general way, one's picture of change, with all its conditions and forms, may be based on various doctrinal movements which tend to fall into antithetical pairs as follows:
— a monistic (materialist or spiritual) view of causality or a pluralistic one (according a relative autonomy to various historical series);
— a linear or cyclical view of history, as advanced respectively by Condorcet and Vico;
— an optimistic or pessimistic approach to the future, as for example in the cases of Marx or Spengler respectively.
At a much more specific level, we find work on changes which have taken place in the course of recent decades. Related, as the case may be, to research

of a basically sociological or basically psychological kind, such work tries to define the nature of the exogenous or endogenous factors of change and of the agents of innovation and its spread.

For example, in seeking to explain certain changes which took place in the French education system between 1950 and 1980 (notably the increase in the numbers of secondary school pupils and the abandonment of literary streams in favour of scientific ones), M. Cherkaoui ascribes more importance to the endogenous factors (such as social image and the advantages which individuals expected to derive from their studies) than to the exogenous ones such as the increase in population or reform of the education system. In other words, the rate of (i.e. the increase in) the number of persons choosing the scientific streams would be a function of the benefit hoped for by each group or sub-group. 'Psychologically and socially,' states Cherkaoui, 'there is a higher rate of participation in the élite represented by the mathematical stream in the case of sons of middle-class families, threatened by downward social mobility, than in the case of sons or particularly daughters of working-class families, whose social trajectory is upwards'[1]. It will be seen how difficult it is to separate the endogenous factors from the exogenous one of socio-professional status. Moreover, we may ask whether the difference in the view of the future as between one social class and another is reduceable to purely psychological factors.

Among short-term studies, it may be interesting to draw attention to one by A.M. Huberman on the causes of educational innovation[2]. According to this author, 'the main factor appears to be the relative importance attached to the anticipated advantages and threats of the change in the eyes of the persons affected'. For example, teachers have a tendency to oppose all change which tends to reduce their authority over their classes. Thus Huberman's theories appear to approach those of Cherkaoui. However, while stressing the importance of psychological features common to those who initiate and those who accept innovation, such as self-confidence and the tendency to accept risks, Huberman points to the weight of institutional or social factors such as financial support, the level of teacher training and the socio-cultural origin of the students.

Between these two extremes of very broad concepts and empirical, short-term research, there is a whole gamut of different theories on the relationship between social change and change in education. The variety and even irreconcilability of these theories obliges us to consider the problem of change, with all its mechanisms and factors, as an open one. This unavoidably open approach does not prevent us from formulating certain general propositions concerning the organization and relative ranking of the factors of change.

The interplay of these factors will be more specifically defined in Chapters VI and VII.

Let us recall that in the chapters which go to make up this second part of our study, the accent will more often be on the conditions of change in education than on its functions and effects.

Two paradigms of change: equilibrium and conflict

In sketching out a typology of present-day concepts of social and educational change, R.G. Paulston uses the notion of the paradigm, defined by T.S. Kuhn as 'the way a scientific/professional community views a field of study, identifies appropriate problems for study, and specifies legitimate concepts and methods'.

Paulston has selected two paradigms[3]: the equilibrium paradigm, which is the older; and the more recent conflict paradigm. Four theories attach to each of these paradigms. Paulston's distinction has been taken up in a recent work on the 'production' functions of the school. The author, A. Petitat, compares *functionalist* theories, which accord particular importance to the problem of social integration, and *conflictualist* theories which place class conflict and dominance relations at the centre of the historical stage. At the end of his analysis, the author considers that 'all theoretical constructions whatsoever are built up around the functional or the functional-conflictual principle of their contribution to reproduction of the social order, social integration or class domination'. He also criticizes the pretention of these theories to universality, emphasizing the need to distinguish various rhythms in the evolution of the educational system. In this connection, while the educational authorities serve the powers-that-be in the short term, they may also in the long run be unconsciously contributing to its ruin[4].

The equilibrium paradigm

In seeking an explanation to the process of change, the *evolutionist and neo-evolutionist theories* base themselves on the contributions of biology and on the ideas of progress and stages of development. Change is assimilated to progress towards greater social and cultural differentiation and specialization. In order to maintain the stability of the whole, the education system has to adapt to this process.

Basing themselves on the results of ethnological research and taking the effects of decolonization into account, the new evolutionists recognize cultural diversity and consider change as a multilinear progress and not as a simple development process of universal validity. In this connection, the efforts of certain Third World countries to reform their education system have led them to call the models supplied by the industrialized countries into question and to conceive new educational policies.

The *structural-functional theory* stresses the slow and cumulative nature of change while according due importance to the homeostatic mechanisms without which a society would be unable to survive. The factors of change can only be exterior to the system. Thus, any internal conflict is considered as pathological. The functionalists are thus led to accept social inequality in which they perceive the necessary condition for maintenance of the existing order. As regards the relations between the school and society, if the former depends on the latter for its resources and the legitimation of its status, society also depends on the school which, in continuing the task of socialization begun by the family, ensures continuity between successive generations.

The *systems theory* takes up certain aspects of the structural-functional theory in order to explain, on the one hand, the relations which grow up inside the education system; and, on the other, the links which bind the system to the socio-economic context. However, this theory attempts to overcome certain difficulties encountered by the functionalists, as when it considers dysfunction of the system as a possible source of the need for change.

To some extent it would be possible to relate structuralist concepts to these last two theories of change. In this respect, let us consider the structuralist interpretation of the educational practices of ancient Sparta. The *cryptia* was a period of initiation in the course of which the young Spartan from the élite class lived isolated in the mountains, secretly killing helots or serfs. According to the classical theory, the object of the *cryptia* was to prepare the young man for the life of a hoplite or adult infantryman. However, in a contribution to a collective work entitled *Structure sociale et histoire*[5], P. Vidal-Naquet shows that the structuralist concept supplies a new analytical framework. It stresses antimonical relations uniting the *cryptia* (e.g. nakedness, isolation, life in the mountains) and the hoplite heavily armed and fighting in groups on the plains. On one side there is nature and disorder; on the other culture and order. Such a structure can only be abolished by external factors such as the enlargement of the Greek world and evolution of the technique of war. If the structuralists have aided the historians to escape from their 'Eurocentricity', declares M. Rébérioux with regard to this approach, the latter accuse the former of emphasizing the notion of stability whereas historical analysis prefers that of change[6]. For structuralists, explains A. Soboul, 'the motive force behind the growth and disappearance of structures is essentially external, for example war or accident. Historical analysis sees this force as primarily internal, in the form of contradiction'[7].

The conflict paradigm
Contradiction – notably the tension between the old and the new – thus becomes a primary subject of historical investigation.

We know, in this connection, that the schoolbooks issued by the French Revolution of 1789 taught new ideas in a traditional framework, namely that of the religious catechism. The conflict sometimes takes the form of a confrontation between two ideologies or two types of rationality. Thus, in France at the beginning of the twentieth century, the threat that the teacher training colleges, which were considered to attract insufficient numbers, might be suppressed, led the association of lecturers in these establishments to bring up two types of argument against the ministerial project of 'redistribution' of means: (a) the need to satisfy the educational needs of the departments; and (b) the importance of keeping classes in the training colleges small so as to achieve better training of teachers[8].

According to C.F. Kaestle, the historian should take an interest in different types of conflict and study their interactions. Apart from conflicts between groups or social classes, there are others which arise inside groups and others again within the life of each individual. While the author refuses to reduce religious, ethnic, geographical or institutional conflicts to the level of class conflict, he considers that one can only speak of pluralist society if the terms of one type of conflict (for example, between church and State) do not necessarily coincide with those of another type, such as social struggle or university competition. In other words, within any framework of selection, the non-pluralist society would tolerate or legitimize the substitution of irrelevant criteria for relevant ones, this substitution being rendered possible by the established confusion between professional competence on the one hand and, on the other, the ideological, political, ethnic, psychological or moral characteristics of the individuals or groups concerned.

As to the modes of resolving conflicts, Kaestle advocates compromise. Evoking the education of immigrants at the end of the last century, he begins by underlining the ambiguity of the role of the school, which undeniably tends to strangle the culture of the immigrants, thus alienating children from their parents. At the same time, however, it constituted a powerful instrument of introduction to American life. Thus the author concludes that families were in the last resort right to send their children to school[9].

According to Paulston, the conflict paradigm is illustrated by four theoretical movements: Marxism, neo-Marxism, the cultural revitalization theory and the utopian or anarchist movement.

Marxism, according to G. Bois, emerges 'as a general theory of movement in society which it attempts to explain by the use of a number of specific tools or basic concepts, among which the first is that of the means of production'[10]. Whether as a philosophical theory in the form of dialectical materialism, or as a social theory in the form of historical materialism, Marxism is far from having achieved universal recognition. Furthermore, certain dogmatic distortions have led many to contest its scientific or heuristic value. At the same time, these distortions have given rise to attempts to restate the theory. Thus, 'the name covers widely differing historical approaches which are sometimes even quite foreign to one another'[11].

However, a certain number of general principles or intellectual attitudes are common to all those claiming to be Marxists: a desire to construct an overall version of history simultaneously taking into account the economic, mental, social and political aspects of existence; a tendency to confer a key role on the class struggle; and a preoccupation with according priority to structures before events and to the collective before the individual. These principles and attitudes exert an indirect influence on many historians who, as the case may be, play up the role of economic elements, analyse the function of ideologies, or emphasize the importance of the notion of conflict.

New problems are raised by those stemming most directly from Marxism: for example, how is it possible to reconcile the apparently dominant rule of some particular element of the superstructure of a given society, such as religion or politics, with the theory of the ultimate dominance of the means of production and the priority given to infrastructures[12]?

Essential notions such as that of the 'working class' lose some of their importance or alter as a function of the complexity of the system of production. In this connection, M. Verret considers that the manufacture of an industrial product cannot be exclusively attributed to those who worked on it directly. Other employees also produce added value. Hence, 'the essential criterion of distinction becomes position within the system of authority'[13].

As regards the place of human beings in history, the position taken in 1888 by Engels in *Ludwig Feuerbach* is well known: 'the objects of action are desired, but their real results are not; or, if at first they seem to correspond to the end in view, they have final consequences quite different from those intended'. This reflection throws light on the reversal effects of which the history of education supplies us with many examples. Thus, in carrying out its double (economic and ideological) function – to lead pupils to recognize the rightness or the immutability of social structures – the school is led simultaneously to teach certain subjects and to inhibit the exercise of critical judgement[14]. But in the more or less long run, the teaching of these subjects can cause unintended effects such as the raising of doubts concerning the ideological objectives originally assigned to the school.

The importance of these reversal effects and the variety of development processes lead certain Marxist historians and philosophers simultaneously to reject any causal explanation of a mechanical kind and any universal and teleological theory of the evolution of societies[15]. Others, having condemned historicism, go still further in proposing to renew the notion of progress. This historicism has been defined by Popper as 'a theory relating to all social sciences which makes historical prediction their main aim, and which foresees that this end can be attained if one succeeds in discovering the "rhythms" or the "patterns", the "laws" or the "general trends" underlying historical developments'. Such authors hold that 'for Marxism the idea of progress is first and foremost embodied in a refusal of, a resistance to all forms of oppression and exploitation'[16].

There is nothing fantastic in the idea of a Marxist notion of progress which would be founded on an apprenticeship in social contradictions, independent of any systematic projection into the future. In this case, Marxism is imagined not in terms of a doctrine of power, but rather as the first possibility offered to humanity of resisting the crushing power of society by attempting to understand it and to place oneself within it[17].

If we refer to Marx's own ideas on education we find, on the one hand, that the school is seen as playing a role in the building up of the workforce and in the inculcation of the dominant ideology; and, on the other, that importance is attributed to an early association of education and labour, this link being seen as 'one of the most powerful means of transforming present-day society'[18].

Among the other approaches which Paulston classifies under the conflict paradigm, the cultural revitalization theory places the emphasis not on the role of social classes, but on the deliberate, conscious and organized efforts of groups (for example prophetic, ethnic or revolutionary movements) to construct a more satisfactory culture. It implies the rejection of public instruction as an instrument of acculturation, and the project of creating new schools. Referring to various movements such as that of P. Freire, the proponents of this theory consider that individuals can only be motivated if they are personally involved in the process of change. In consequence, they ask educators to associate themselves with groups or communities which they consider as the main agents of educational change.

Finally, historians of the utopian or anarchist school play their part in the general debate on educational change, criticize socio-economic realities and dream of the creation of a better world. But they are cautious about putting ideas into practice, or even supporting their point of view with evidence taken from the social sciences. Nevertheless, they do sometimes propose measures such as abolition of the monopoly of the school, its opening to life and the redistribution of educational resources in favour of the under-privileged.

In his conclusion, Paulston evaluates the significance of the various theories or studies of change. In this respect, few studies succeed in grasping the nature of power in the carrying out of educational reform, whether with regard to the successive political, administrative or research and development phases of such action. Similarly, there has not been enough research on the evaluation of the short- and long-term effects of reform. Paulston therefore recommends an increase in systematic comparative studies on the results of reform in its political or socio-economic context, from different theoretical points of view (the equilibrium or the conflict paradigm)[19].

While it would appear futile to try to find precise answers to all the questions which have emerged in the course of presenting the various theories of change, it is on the other hand possible to make some general comments on factors leading to change and their relative importance.

A 'multifactorial' conception of causality

In fact, it is just as necessary to speak of factors tending to ensure stability or permanence as of factors of change, inasmuch as the process of historical research, being based on the in-depth study of contexts, consists of looking alternately at the past and the present in order to distinguish both continuities and differences.

Thus, the law according official recognition to the trade unions in France represented both an apparent return to the associations and corporations dissolved in 1791 and a promise of liberation for the working class. It was indeed on account of the law's ambiguous character that both conservative and progressive deputies voted for it in 1884.

One could generalize this observation by considering that an educational event usually calls for the simultaneous involvement of several factors. Let us consider several examples illustrating this 'multifactorial' conception of causality:

— Under the *ancien régime*, the larger increase in the number of colleges between 1560 and 1610 arose from the combination of three forces, namely the royal power, the city bourgeoisie (who saw in secondary education an essential element in the social ascent of their children), and the churches, who viewed the college as an instrument of Protestant or Catholic reform[20].

— The voting of laws on compulsory education in France in the second half of the nineteenth century corresponded to the conjunction of different, and even contradictory interests, namely those of the authorities who saw in the school an instrument of control and moralization, of the future republican élite who wanted to extract the working classes from the clutches of the clergy, and finally of the people themselves, whose demands in the matter of education will be analysed in the following chapter[21].

— The growth years in the development of adult education courses in nineteenth-century France seem to have been determined by increased rural-urban migration, favourable economic circumstances and an upsurge in the labour movement[22].

The refusal of what the historian Marc Bloch called the 'monism' in causation goes together with rejection of a unilateral view of the causal relation. In other words, the same educational phenomenon may, according to the case, act as either cause or effect. Let us go back to the example of the establishment of adult education courses in the nineteenth century. By helping to reduce the rate of illiteracy, these courses influenced, in their turn, not only economic and social development but also their own. In effect, they have to be adapted to satisfy the new requirements of a public which, thanks to them, has reached a certain level of education.

Since the factors of change are both numerous and linked by complex relationships, is it possible to rank them? No absolute answer can be given to such a question. Any answer must depend on the chosen subject, the period in question and also the progress of research. Thus, in the history of adult education in France at the end of the nineteenth century, ideological and political factors appear to take primacy before economic and social ones. At that time the confrontations between lay and Christian movements, stirred up by the application of the school laws, gave rise to a competitive situation which, in its turn, stimulated a process of educational homogenization and innovation[23]. A further example, taken from the field of electoral geography, suggests reasons why the ranking of factors in the hierarchy cannot lead to the application of any universal model.

In order to explain the stability of voting in different parts of France, A. Siegfried contrasted areas where land was owned or held on a large scale and where the peasants voted like the landowners with areas where smallholdings were typical, which were considered as pillars of democracy. In 1960 this theory was contested by P. Bois who, in studying the department of Sarthe in greater depth, showed that the decisive factor was less the scale of property than the manner in which the land which had been put up for sale during the course of the Revolution had been acquired. For example, in the west of the Sarthe where the generally rich lands had been purchased by bourgeois buyers, the frustrated peasants identified the Revolution with the bourgeoisie and themselves joined forces with the nobility. In the east, by contrast, where the land was poor and where, in the course of seeking outlets for their artisanal production, the peasant weavers were in permanent contract with the towns, the political situation was quite different. Reviewing more recent research on the stability of electoral behaviour, T. Zeldin notes the part played by the modalities of urban penetration into rural areas and to psychological and moral factors; for example, the counter-revolution had often been the work of persons seeking to satisfy their personal ambitions, to gratify local desires for revenge or to escape conscription[24].

Thus we observe a network of economic, social and individual factors, all with a bearing on behaviour the persistence of which eludes any simple and unilateral determinism.

As regards individual factors, there is a frequent tendency to consider a person or a political authority responsible for taking a decision as an individual or group which, acting in a rational manner, is fully aware of the immediate and long-term consequences. But the nature of this rationality often only appears when application of the decision reveals the importance of the political, economic or social stakes. For example, a plan to initiate educational reform or to create some educational institution may at first be no more than the result of humanitarian tendencies or of a prestige-seeking policy. Subsequently, the carrying out of the project or analysis of the initial results may bring about the intervention of different social or political forces, giving rise to new motivations and new factors at stake.

In history, as in sociology or psychology, the attempt to identify and rank the factors of change may give rise to hasty generalizations when the analysis is limited to situations which are 'favoured' from the research point of view. For example, the importance of biological factors in certain diagnoses of debility or dyslexia cannot justify the tendency to consider them preponderantly, if not exclusively, responsible for all forms of educational retardation. The same applies to sociology, where the study of certain groups such as ethnic minorities or sub-proletarian layers of the population may lead researchers to put forward conclusions regarding the decisive influence of social factors to other groups.

In history, an interest in some particular public, for example boarding-school pupils or the children of fringe groups, or the preferential use of a given source, such as the point of view of the authorities, also tends to lead to a one-sided view of the functions of the school.

To sum up, ranking of factors of change is an open problem, and particularly if the questions are put in too general terms, thus eliciting responses in which it is difficult to find the distinction between ideology and demonstration. It should be added that historical research can help to solve this problem by taking as its object precisely the relation between scientific method and ideological intrusion in the development of an idea or an educational practice.

We shall be returning to the interplay of the factors of change in the coming chapters in the course of reviewing subjects, currently very topical in historiography, such as literacy, popular education and teaching techniques.

NOTES AND REFERENCES

1. Cherkaoui, M. *Les changements du système éducatif en France, 1950–1980*. Paris, Presses universitaires de France, 1982, p. 225.
2. Huberman, A.M. *Understanding change in education: an introduction*. Paris, Unesco: IBE, 1973, p. 92.
3. Paulston, R.G. Social and educational change: conceptual frameworks. *Comparative education review* (Chicago, IL), vol. 21, nos. 2/3, June/October 1977, p. 370–395.
4. Petitat, A. *Production de l'école. Production de la société*. Geneva, Librairie Droz, 1982. 540 p.
5. Labrousse, E. Structure sociale et histoire. *Raison présente* (Paris), no. 7, 1968, p. 41–72.
6. Ibid.
7. Ibid.
8. *Bulletin trimestriel de l'Association amicale des professeurs des écoles normales d'instituteurs et des écoles normales d'institutrices de France*, no. 1, 1903, p. 13–51.
9. Kaestle, C.F. Conflict and consensus revisited: notes toward a reinterpretation of American educational history. *Harvard educational review* (Cambridge, MA, Harvard University), vol. 46, no. 3, August 1976, p. 390–396.
10. Bois, G. Marxisme et histoire nouvelle. *In:* Le Goff, J., ed. *La nouvelle histoire*. Paris, Retz, 1978, p. 375.
11. Ibid., p. 376.
12. Ibid.

13. Boudon, R. et al. Méthodologie et épistémologie. *L'année sociologique* (Paris), 1981, p. 8–17.
14. Milhau, J. *Le marxisme en mouvement.* Paris, Presses universitaires de France, 1975. 184 p.
15. Ibid
16. Gaudeau, G.; Naud, D. Marxisme et progrès. *Raison présente* (Paris), no. 66, 1983, p. 83–95.
17. Ibid.
18. Lê Thành Khôi. *Les idées de Marx sur l'éducation.* Paris, Université de Paris V, 1983. 11p.
19. Paulston, R.G., *Op. cit.*
20. Compère, Marie-Madeleine; Julia, D. Les collèges sous l'Ancien Régime: présentation d'un instrument de travail. *Histoire de l'éducation* (Paris, Institut national de la recherche pédagogique), no. 13, décembre 1981, p. 1–27.
21. Ozouf, J. Le peuple et l'école: note sur la demande populaire d'instruction en France au XIXᵉ siècle. *In:* Bedarida, P.F., et al. *Mélanges d'histoire sociale offerts à Jean Maitron.* Paris, Les Editions ouvrières, 1976.
22. Léon, A. *Histoire de l'éducation populaire en France.* Paris, Nathan, 1983.
23. Ibid.
24. Zeldin, T. *Histoire des passions françaises, 1848–1945. Vol. 4: Colère et politique.* 3rd ed. Paris, Eds. Recherches, 1979. 424 p.

CHAPTER VI

Literacy and
the popular demand for education

The present controversies on the real power of the school or on the deschooling of society are echoed in research and reinterpretation concerning the forms, factors and functions of literacy in the course of recent centuries. Thus the data gathered at the beginning of the Third Republic by rector L. Maggiolo have been submitted to a new statistical treatment with a view to estimating the evolution of the rate of literacy from the seventeenth century on by counting the number of signatures on acts of marriage.

Joint developments

Although the rate of literacy, which varied considerably according to place, social status and sex, increased as a function of the spread of education, the effect of influences exterior to the school were by no means negligible. In this connection, F. Furet and J. Ozouf lay stress on the role of the church which, quite apart from any system of schooling, dispensed elementary instruction usually limited to reading[1].

From the Middle Ages to the nineteenth century, the transition from limited to general literacy in Western countries is bound up with a number of changes.

Reporting on an international symposium in 1979 on the subject of 'Literacy, social change and development', R. Chartier mentions some of these changes – the end of the monopoly of professional scribes; the institution of an individual relationship to the text; and the dissolution of traditional communities. In addition, the growing use of writing brought about a development of certain intellectual techniques such as the stocking and organization of knowledge, for example in the filing of information and the compiling of lists and tables, etc.[2]. In this connection, A. Petitat evokes the numerous effects ascribed to the small schools of the *ancien régime:*

They attempted to restrain an uncontrolled socialization which inspired fear among the bourgeois élite, sensitized by the emotions of the mob. But this service to the ruling classes was combined with a long-term contribution to the spread of writing, a cultural change of vast consequences, one of which deserves to be mentioned here, namely the emergence of those day labourers, craftsmen and workers who, having acquired the three Rs, henceforward possessed a new tool for the construction of their solidarity and their cultural references ... These schools proved productive at other levels also, contributing to national unification, the opening up of regions, and linguistic unification related to the long-term emergence of nation states[3].

In the course of the same symposium, some historians underlined the degree of correlation, in various parts of Europe from the seventeenth century on, between the rate of literacy and the density of the school network. On the other hand, in certain countries like Sweden, where religious control and family apprenticeships were major elements of society, the increase in literacy appears to have been independent of the education system.

In addition, for the period 1650–1830, J. Houdaille obtained a significant negative correlation by classifying the various regions of France, first according to the rate of literacy and second according to the percentage of men of letters. Houdaille interprets this unexpected result as follows: 'In regions where there is little education, educated persons wield the pen more easily than in those where there are many readers, perhaps because they feel less inhibited by possible competition and because they enjoy relatively greater prestige'[4]. This interpretation raises a question: if, instead of writers', the sample had consisted of scientists, would the result of the statistical analysis have been the same?

Within the framework of research into popular education in the nineteenth century, the present author has shown that to the north-east of a line drawn from Mont-Saint-Michel to Geneva not only was the level of education of conscripts higher than in the regions to the west and south of it, but also that there were more adult education classes per 10,000 inhabitants, a higher proportion of students attending such classes and a better level of results. The coherence of these results is confirmed by statistical evidence which reveals the existence of positive and significant correlations between the ranking of *départements* and data concerning the different elements contributing to literacy[5].

It would appear difficult to establish causal relations between these elements and to state, for example, that the existence of adult education classes was responsible for reducing the amount of illiteracy. On the other hand, there is nothing to stop us pointing out the possible influence of general factors on the education system and the acquistion of literacy. In this connection, if we take an overall look at the geographical distribution of levels of education, various arguments have been advanced to explain the persistence of the dividing line between Mont-Saint-Michel and Geneva. In 1848, Baron Dupin pointed to the role of industrialization, urbanization and socio-economic status (based on taxable income). Other factors that have been taken into account include the extent to which regions were exposed to external influences and the gap between the language of school and the vernacular[6]. Certain authors attach importance to the circulation of written matter within a society; in other words, the decisive progress of literacy during the course of the second half of the nineteenth century would be linked to the development of school libraries and the general use of the school exercise book[7].

At any event, it would seem certain that both past and present factors combined in creating favourable conditions in certain areas for the establishment of schools and adult classes, high proportions of school attendance and satisfactory results.

Under the effects of the school laws of 1881 and 1882, the dividing line gradually blurred and finally disappeared just before the First World War, when the rate of illiteracy fell below 3 per cent.

In effect, at the beginning of the twentieth century, there occurred a sort of reversal of certain secular tendencies. In other words, the south began to overtake the north. There appear to have been several reasons for this change. In the first place, we have the standardizing effects of the application of the compulsory education laws. Demographic differences also played a role: the same resources and the same equipment produce better results in low birth-rate areas, such as the south, than in zones of high population density. Further, we should not neglect the scale of migratory currents from the south to the north, which led the migrants to qualify themselves with a view to finding jobs in the secondary and tertiary sectors of the cities and suburbs[8].

This last phenomenon shows the ambiguity of the idea of the demand for education. In effect, such a demand proceeds partly from the way in which individuals or groups perceive their immediate or future interests, and partly from the means of education and social promotion which they may or may not be offered.

The history and geography of the demand for education

The historical and geographical study of the relation between industrialization and the growth of literacy throws light on the nature of both.

In this connection, C.M. Cipolla has drawn attention to the fact that the rate of literacy in England at the beginning of the Industrial Revolution increased very little. In effect, it passed from 51 per cent in the period 1756–62 to 54 per cent in the period 1799–1804. He also noted the superiority of agricultural areas in the north as compared to industrial ones. In 1851, the rate of literacy had risen to 68 per cent in the agricultural areas, but had stagnated at 51 per cent in Lancashire, the cradle of the Industrial Revolution. This paradox stems partly from the desire of many industrialists to recruit an ever-younger and thus not yet educated workforce, and partly from their fear that the spread of education might lead to the desertion of workers and the propagation of what they considered to be subversive ideas[9]. However, once the economic value of education had been understood, it gave rise to the Factory Act (1802) whereby the wool and cotton magnates were obliged to install classrooms in their factories. Nevertheless, it was not until the middle of the nineteenth century that literacy advanced at the same rate as industrialization.

Phenomena similar to those of Lancashire were observed in the north of France, where the rural cantons had a higher rate of literacy than the industrialized ones[10]. Other phenomena, sometimes unexpected, have been analysed by G. Desert in connection with the progress of literacy during the nineteenth century in the *Grand-Ouest*. To begin with, the quest for more knowledge developed mainly within the framework of similar social structures. In other words, by making way for intermediate categories, such frameworks offered workers greater possibilities of promotion. Furthermore, local enquiries have revealed some paradoxical situations. Thus, in areas such as Normandy, where literacy had been common for a long time, the owners were more educated than their workpeople, whereas in areas such as Brittany, where literacy arrived later, the reverse may be observed. In order to explain this inversion, Desert suggests that the owners were generally older than their workpeople, and thus benefited to a lesser extent from the recent development of literacy. In conclusion, he estimates that 'there exist regional climates with regard to education, climates which at least partly neutralize economic and social influences'[11].

The differences between these 'regional climates' have been studied by M. Netter in connection with the development of primary teaching in the eighteenth and nineteenth centuries in two areas nowadays represented by the *départements* of Haute-Garonne and Yonne. In order to estimate the local demand for education, the author picked out a number of indicators such as the density of the school network, the social status of teachers, the respect or otherwise of prohibitions relating to co-education, and the reaction (or lack of it) to the closing of a school. Analysis of the resulting data has shown the superiority of the Yonne to the Haute-Garonne as regards the enrolment of pupils in schools.

Netter imputes this superiority to dominant social structures and ways of life in the two areas. In the Haute-Garonne, where the land belonged to a small number of large land-owners, the few schools had an élitist character; the opposition of the élite towards mass education was echoed by the resistance by the people towards knowledge considered irrelevant. In the Yonne, on the other hand, where there was an important class of small independent land-owners, there were quite a number of primary schools. These taught pupils the rudiments of reading, writing and arithmetic, considered necessary by parents, without depriving the latter of the workforce they needed during the season of fine weather[12].

Quite apart from regional differences, the working-class demand for education in the nineteenth century ran up against the interests of a bourgeoisie which, without losing sight of the need for social control by the school, proclaimed its attachment to the values of merit and individual success within the framework of general progress. While prominent citizens gladly express their opinions on the functions which the school does or should fulfil, the same is not always true of members of the working classes. However, an analysis of certain studies and eye-witness accounts relating to the nineteenth century has enabled Ozouf to list the various motivations and attitudes underlying popular demand for education[13].

— First and foremost comes the desire for human dignity and the shame of illiteracy, a reaction already perceptible in urban circles during the eighteenth century.
— Next comes the desire to conform to certain models suggested by the upper classes, to have one's children educated, although parents were not necessarily conscious of the social or professional consequences of education.
— There is also an awareness of the usefulness in daily and professional life of being able to write a letter, cope with administrative requirements, do sums, escape from the harshness of rural life or acquire a rank in the armed forces.
— In the nineteenth century, there was also the hope of liberating one's children from the servitude of wage-labouring.
— Finally, with the rise of the labour movement, there was a desire to play a useful part in the social and political struggle.

In conclusion, 'the poor child who succeeds, that central figure of nineteenth-century educational mythology, might very well be for the middle classes the exception which justified the entire system'. But, Ozouf considers, 'for the people, it was a semi-religious collective hope'[14].

The persistence of this image and of this hope, in spite of all the crises which have shaken the different systems of values during the twentieth century, was to aid the survival, if not the success, of the school as an institution. Can these institutions be generally transferred to other cultural or political climates, notably in the countries of the Third World?

Analysing in this context the chances of success of literacy programmes in new countries, A. Meister relates the attitudes and the motivations of those concerned to factors considered essential such as the modernity of the economy, the amount of will-power put into development and the practicality of the education provided. Thus, in a traditional rural situation, characterized by the absence of a will to economic development, the need for literacy is not perceived. By contrast, however, in a rural situation where modernization is in full swing and there is a strong desire for planning, some of the motivations and attitudes evoked above are to be found among the workers, notably the desire to acquire the prestige accorded to those who know how to read, a quest for better earnings and success, etc.

Does this mean that the Third World countries should follow the European model in all that concerns the relationship between education and development? In his book on the subject, Meister rejects any such assimilation. More precisely, after stressing the importance of the 'social fall-out' of literacy (by which he implies a widening of human contacts and familiarization with the world of the mass media), he gives his opinion that, contrary to what happened in Europe, where economic progress brought about social modernization (for example with respect to labour legislation and cultural institutions), in the newly established countries social modernization should precede economic development. In brief, 'the social conflict would be the motive force behind a slow process of economic development'[15].

One could equally well stress the interactions – rather than the relation of cause and effect – linking the two forms of development. The choice of priorities should thus be dictated by the particular circumstances of each country.

Let us now take a look not only at the reactions of manual workers faced with an education programme designed by others, but also at their own contribution to the working out and putting into practice of the principles of popular education.

The workers and popular education

The contribution of the workers, and particularly of the factory workers, to the working out of educational theory and practice has given rise to three kinds of study dealing respectively with the older forms of popular culture, the development of popular education during the nineteenth century, and finally the notion of technical culture. This notion will be analysed in the following chapter, when we come to consider the concepts of the cultural object and cultural behaviour.

With respect to the traditional forms of popular culture, as opposed to aristocratic or middle-class culture, R. Mandrou reminds us of the necessary distinction between works created by the people and those created for them by other social classes. The literature sold by pedlars, about which this author has written a book, occupies a special position in relation to both, since on the one hand the works sold as the *Bibliothèque bleue de Troyes* were written by workers in the printing trade, and on the other hand the pedlars were able to keep the publisher informed about popular demand, thus orienting production[16]. Analysis of the content of peddled books enables us to identify the main subjects of popular culture under the *ancien régime*. They included mythology, religion and the representation of society. Thus, texts relating to the world of work lay much stress on the poverty of the apprentices or on the servitude inherent in working journeyman, but never refer to rivalries between guilds or to social antagonisms.

Apart from the production and consumption of specific works, R. Muchembled holds that popular culture conveyed both a certain vision of the world and certain kinds of collective behaviour[17]. This vision and this behaviour are understood indirectly for the period between the fifteenth and the eighteenth centuries thanks to analysis of the sentences pronounced by the courts of church and State against the agents of popular culture. It must be said that the popular conscience at that time held a magical and animist view of the world, engendered by a climate of insecurity and fear. This view favoured the hold of sorcery over society, giving rise to sometimes explosive games and feasts tending to reinforce family and village solidarity. One can understand that these practices were intolerable both to official religion and to the centralizing and standardizing policy of the kings. Muchembled tells us that 'in the seventeenth and eighteenth centuries, the repression of popular culture, which was carried out deliberately in the name of religious and political values, prepared the ground for the dominance of the cities, for the progress of science and for learned culture'.

Particularly in the Scandinavian countries, the traditional forms of popular culture for a long time acted as non-scholastic channels for the transmission of knowledge. L. Musset tells us that at the end of the Middle Ages, the ordinary language of the people in these countries served for the writing of historical accounts (even official ones), technical treatises and religious poetry[18].

Some traditional forms of popular education, such as peddled literature, feasts and vigils, survived into the nineteenth century. At that time, however, they came to be dominated by a vast movement of popular education which, embracing reading-rooms, courses for adults, school libraries and classes for apprentices, tried to find answers to the new economic, social, demographic or political problems caused by the industrialization of the European countries. The movement was sustained either by the State, which was the main organizer of adult courses, or by leading citizens who, by means of lay or confessional associations, took it upon themselves to provide moral training for youth, and to shelter it from the temptations of the street and the influence of what was considered to be subversive propaganda.

How should we define the relation between the labour movement and popular education in nineteenth-century France[19]?

One might begin by saying that by its very existence, by its struggles, by the threat which it was supposed to represent to good order and social peace, the labour movement incited the State, the Church and leading citizens to set up instruments of control, among which popular education takes its place.

However, this overall influence in no way exhausts the list of relations which we can draw up between popular education and the labour movement. Thus, it proved possible to encourage the workers to follow adult education courses in response to the new strategies of the movement which, from the 1830s on, seemed to give priority to education and propaganda before violent action.

Moreover, in their capacity as students at adult education courses or consumers of other forms of popular education, the workers contributed, by their expectations and reactions, to the evolution of the education they were receiving by rejecting content and methods considered to be excessively academic or by refusing the moralizing and didactic works to be found in popular editions.

If we now consider the role of the militants as such, those whose lives are cited in the biographical dictionary of J. Maitron[20], we can speak of the working out of specific and original forms of working-class self-education. Following the legalization of the trade unions in 1884, this self-education went ahead within the framework of labour exchanges where evening courses were developed partly along the lines of the public adult education courses. Nevertheless, the introduction of specific subjects such as labour legislation and the history of the labour movement made these courses an instrument of trade union education.

Well before the legalization of the trade unions and the setting up of labour exchanges, the self-education of the working class had developed two particular forms: 'mutualism' and the reading of newspapers edited by the workers themselves.

The mutualist model, which is still found in the organization of some elementary schools, presupposes the pooling of the intellectual and affective resources of a group with a view to creating a suitable climate for the advent of a society free from segregation and élitism. It was, indeed, doubly significant in that it implied both mutual assistance among the workers and independence from other social classes.

As for the workers' press, which had its beginnings in the 1830s, it was a weapon which represented a particular form of popular education. Though they sometimes expressed different opinions on important matters such as élitism or collaboration with the authorities, the workers' newspapers appear to have fulfilled certain common functions such as the following[21]:

— For the workers, to write represented both a claim to equality *vis-à-vis* other social classes and an occasion to show that the mastery of language justified this claim.

— To write was also to affirm the identity of the working class by drawing attention to its struggle, its sufferings and its hopes.

— The workers' press was a vehicle for the denunciation of paternalism and for decoding the socially and morally edifying speeches of important citizens. Thus, in the course of a banquet organized by socialist workers at the end of 1848, a jewellery worker 'proposed a toast to property, not to the kind of property which is the fruit of parasitism, but to the true, morally justified kind of property resulting from work'.

— Finally, the workers' press was a means of mobilization and struggle towards the creation of a new society ruled by association and co-operation.

Any systematic account of the contributions of the labour movement to popular education should give special prominence to the role of socialist theoreticians and of the worker-writers who, in their autobiographies, revealed the difficulties of a worker's relationship to school and learning.

As for the real militants, their influence was not limited simply to the imagining of certain forms of workers' education. It would appear that they took an active part in working out the main theoretical and practical forms of universal education in the nineteenth century.

Thus, particularly towards the end of the century, the ideas of mutualism, association, organization and solidarity, which occupied such an important place in labour thought and action, were embodied in the working of post-school institutions. In addition, they were the basis of the solidarist philosophy which, at this time, inspired many official declarations and debates on popular education.

One certainly cannot speak of any direct influence of one group on another, nor even of any real exchanges between the representatives of the workers' movement and the officials who promoted the different sectors of post-school education. The failure of the people's universities demonstrates the difficulty of such meetings. However, the principles of association and solidarity, which draw a large part of their force from the conditions and forms of economic, social and political life, appear to have imposed themselves first and foremost on the workers' organizations. It is therefore permissible to think that the labour movement was able to arouse ideas and practices inspired by these same principles, either by simple imitation or by the spirit of competition.

Thus it was by taking part in the construction and propagation of social and cultural models that the labour movement contributed to the development of popular education.

This being so, it is reasonable to water down the tendency to ascribe practically all educational theories or achievements to the philosophy of the initiative of the ruling class. At the same time, it is fair to speak of the active and competitive role of working-class culture *vis-à-vis* the dominant culture of the period.

Furthermore, institutions and practices originally designed for the working class subsequently spread to other social groups. The transition from the popular education of the nineteenth century to the lifelong education of

the twentieth illustrates, among other things, this process of extension and transfer[22].
The analysis of certain aspects of the evolution of technical education will lead us to generalize regarding this process.

NOTES AND REFERENCES

1. Furet, F.; Ozouf, J. *Lire et écrire: l'alphabétisation des Français de Calvin à Jules Ferry.* Paris, Ed. de Minuit, 1977. 2 v.
2. Chartier, R. Alphabétisation, changement social et développement. *Bulletin de la Fondation Maison des sciences de l'Homme* (Paris), no. 30, 1979, p. 35–41.
3. Petitat, A. *Production de l'école. Production de la société.* Geneva, Librairie Droz, 1982. 540 p.
4. Houdaille, J. Alphabétisme et genèse des grands hommes. *Population* (Paris, Institut national d'études démographiques), no. 3, 1978, p. 730–736.
5. Léon, A. *Histoire de l'éducation populaire en France.* Paris, Nathan, 1983.
6. Dupeux, G. *La société française, 1789–1970.* 8e éd. Paris, Colin, 1976. 272 p.
7. Chartier, R. *Op. cit.*
8. Lamoure, J. La scolarisation en France: de fortes inégalités régionales. *L'orientation scolaire et professionelle* (Paris, Institut national d'étude du travail et d'orientation professionnelle), vol. 11, no. 3, 1982, p. 195–213.
9. Cipolla, C.M. *Literacy and development in the West.* Harmondsworth, United Kingdom, Penguin Books, 1969.
10. Marchand, P. *Le travail des enfants aux XIXᵉ siècle dans le département du Nord.* Lille, France, Centre régional de documentation pédagogique, 1980.
11. Desert, G. Alphabétisation et scolarisation dans le Grand-Ouest au XIXᵉ siècle. *In: The making of Frenchmen: current directions in the history of education in France, 1679–1979.* Waterloo, Ont., Historical Reflections Press, 1980.
12. Netter, M. *La genèse de la demande populaire d'instruction en milieu rural et ses liens avec la politique scolaire (XVIIIᵉ–début XIXᵉ siècle).* Paris, Association internationale d'histoire de l'éducation, 1981. 12 p.
13. Ozouf, J. Le peuple et l'école: note sur la demande populaire d'instruction en France au XIXᵉ siècle. *In: Bedarida, P.F., et al. Mélanges d'histoire sociale offerts à Jean Maitron.* Paris, Les Editions Ouvrières, 1976.
14. Ibid.
15. Meister, A. *Alphabétisation et développement: le rôle de l'alphabétisation fonctionnelle dans le développement économique et la modernisation.* Paris, Anthropos, 1973, p. 266.
16. Mandrou, R. *De la culture populaire aux XVIIᵉ et XVIIIᵉ siècles.* Paris, Stock, 1965, p. 224.
17. Muchembled, R. *Culture populaire et culture des élites dans la France moderne, XVᵉ–XVIIIᵉ siècle.* Paris, Flammarion, 1978. 400 p.
18. Musset, L. L'éducation dans le monde scandinave jusqu'au XVIᵉ siècle. *In: Mialaret, G.; Vial, J., eds. Histoire mondiale de l'éducation.* Paris, Presses universitaires de France, 1981, v. 1, p. 323–331.
19. Léon, A. *Op. cit.*
20. Maitron, J. *Dictionnaire biographique du mouvement ouvrier français.* Paris, Les Editions ouvrières, 1964.
21. Faure, A.; Rancière, J. *La parole ouvrière, 1830–1851.* Paris, Union générale d'édition, 1976. 448 p.
22. Léon, A. *Op. cit.*

CHAPTER VII

Technical education and culture

For many years technical education and other disciplines considered to be of minor importance, such as physical education, did not attract the attention of many historians. Today this has changed, and they occupy a special place in the history of education.

Research into strictly didactic material can enrich the study of institutions, functions and social groups. Thus, in a recent work on the history and teaching of technical draughtsmanship, Y. Deforge shows that the evolution of graphics, characterized by the transition from the figurative to the semi-figurative and then to the symbolic style, was partly due to changes in methods and conditions of production. For example, the increase in the scale of buildings from the sixteenth century on brought about changes in working methods and gave rise to the application of three-dimensional or descriptive geometry the spread of which, in its turn, had an impact on technical draughtsmanship[1].

The present interest in the history of technical education stems partly from the continuing prejudice against it and partly from the subsequent difficulties in recruiting and training pupils.

In this connection, on the basis of educational psychology, the present author has been led to stress the importance of similarities between the school curriculum and the work really done in the factory on the one hand, and, on the other, the existence of different views and attitudes as between general and technical education. This difference is reflected just as much in the behaviour of teachers as in that of pupils. For example, both tend to think of the relations between classroom and workshop in a unilateral way; a given subject must always be studied first in the former before being practised in the latter[2].

In explaining these contradictions and the difficulties of technical teaching, one is led back to the role of stereotypes which had their origin in the distant past and which are projected on to modern society.

As regards the past, contemporary behaviour can often be traced back to certain attitudes or images which have existed since ancient times. In this connection we remember that, inasmuch as it presupposed an imperfect and unfinished reality, activity concerned with material things was regarded as base in comparison with the nobility of the ideal and of the cosmic perfection which it was supposed to reflect. In addition, since such activity took the form of servile work, it became an object of contempt similar to that in which slave labour was held.

In this we see the beginnings of a sort of amalgam where distinctions between human activities were extended to those who practised them and then, indirectly, to the corresponding educational institutions[3].

However, one cannot reduce the history of technical education to a mere recognition of the recurrent nature of this amalgam. We also need to cast light on the stages and processes by which technical teaching was built up in order to understand the functions which it nowadays performs. Such a project presupposes that the place of technical education within the framework of educational institutions and methods as a whole should first be defined.

Sectors and levels of technical education

If the notion of technical education were simply assimilated to various forms of vocational initiation and training, it could be applied to the educational system of all countries throughout the ages. Thus, the mediæval universities, with their three higher faculties of law, medicine and theology, undoubtedly had a vocational orientation. Similarly, throughout the Middle Ages and down into modern times, corporations and trade guilds saw to the vocational training of craftsmen. One can even go so far as to say that, in the short or the long run, any general education prepares pupils for the world of work.

A comparative study of the different systems of technical education would reveal important differences and an overall sameness. Thus, with regard to the training of skilled workers, it appears that European countries tend to adopt a mixed or dualistic approach combining the school and the factory rather than exclusively scholastic or exclusively practical methods.

If we look at the situation in France, we can define the field of technical education by reference to four criteria. The term implies training:
— given in a public or private school and not in the workshop;
— containing both general and vocational elements, the latter including draughtsmanship, engineering and workshop instruction;
— specifically and directly linked to certain requirements of the task or trade concerned;
— relating to the agricultural, industrial and commercial sectors of economic life, in other words to the production and exchange of goods.

Inside an establishment corresponding to these criteria, the expression 'technical education' designates the group of subjects other than those described as general. These include draughtsmanship, engineering and workshop practice.

Even thus hedged and defined, 'technical education' represents a motley grouping. In effect, one must take into account the seniority of its various branches, and also of its different levels (e.g. workers, technicians, engineers, etc.), of different branches of economic life and of the various ministries responsible for it.

The expression 'technical education' or 'education through work' stems from the idea of pioneers of 'the new education', such as Dewey, Kerchensteiner, Makarenko, Pistrak and Freinet, that manual work can have formative and cultural value.

Finally, the terms 'technological training' or 'technological education' spring from the desire to attach due value to technical training, to underline its intellectual side and to integrate it into the general education system.

This rapid review of the concept of technical training and related notions concerns the situation in France at the present time. Its distinctions and cleavages are the product of French history. If we consider the case of the United Kingdom, the place accorded to technical training in the school system and the relations between general education and apprenticeship varied greatly from one political party to another up to the end of the First World War. Whereas the Conservatives tended to reduce the content of the training to strictly vocational matters, the Liberals wanted technical training linked to secondary education, whereas the Labour Party rejected the idea of early apprenticeship while nevertheless stressing the educational role of technical training[4].

Whatever the relations envisaged or existing between general and vocational education, in every country the technical education system contains different levels for workers, technicians and engineers. The existence of this stratification makes it difficult to discuss the prejudices against technical training, its lower standing or its status as a 'poor relation', in overall terms. In the case of France, can one say that the fate of a student of the *Ecole polytechnique* is unenviable? And this question calls up another: has not the main function of this prestigious institution always been, in accordance with the ambition of its founders, to train specialists in various professions on the basis of a common general curriculum[5]? The analysis of evolutionary trends in the French system of technical training will throw light on the functions it fulfils and, by the same token, enable us to reply to this question. To speak of analysing trends is to affirm the possibility of identifying certain empirical continuities, certain structures or procedures common to different periods. In this connection, let us remember that historical research can be both objective in the way in which it replies to specific questions and subjective, or ideologically oriented, in its way of interrogating reality and in its attempt to construct intelligible views of the whole.

Instead of the word 'trend' some authors prefer the notion of 'evolutionary law', by which they mean the possibility of deducing a constant tendency on the basis of an undenied one. They also propose the notion of a 'law of repetition' with regard to the relation between the given situation and the given consequence[6].

Two 'tendential laws' throw light on the construction of the system of technical training in France.

First trend: a downward current

In accordance with the intellectualist and élitist ideal which appears to have permeated the construction of the entire French education system, technical education was developed from the top down. In other words, whereas the highest level, more theoretical and more difficult of access, was instituted in the course of the second half of the eighteenth century, the middle and lowest levels were established respectively at the end of the nineteenth and towards the middle of the twentieth centuries. It should be added that these chronological points of reference correspond neither to 'origins' nor to 'first creations' but to real attempts to systematize an institution and make it generally available.

1. The upper level

Without losing sight of certain doctrinal or institutional anticipations, one can reasonably say that the beginnings of higher technical education were contemporary with the Encyclopaedia. Among other establishments created at that time, let us mention the *Ecole des Ponts et Chaussées* (1747), the *Ecole des Mines* (1783) and the *Ecole polytechnique* (1794). The rise of higher technical education took place in an economic, technical and ideological context characterized notably by the transition from the 'eotechnical' to the 'palaeotechnical' phase (according to L. Mumford, the former phase was characterized by the use of water as a source of energy and of wood as a material while, during the latter, coal and iron took the place of water and wood); by the emergence of a new approach associating the idea of usefulness to the desire for knowledge; and by the rehabilitation of manual work.

With the exception of schools of draughtsmanship, this rehabilitation did not lead to any development of elementary technical education. The production system continued to be predominantly artisanal and any attempt to broaden popular education generally came up against objections or outright refusal on the part of the aristocracy and the middle classes.

Let us take the case of the *Ecole polytechnique*, whose functions appear to continue those of the schools of engineers under the *ancien régime*. On the

basis of statistics relating to the first thirty years (1794–1824) in the life of this establishment, we have shown that over 10 per cent of the students subsequently had careers in fields other than the military or engineering[7], for example administration, education or politics.

In his recent book on the recruitment and subsequent careers of *'polytechniciens'*, T. Shinn considers that the upper-middle classes were overrepresented at the *Ecole polytechnique* throughout the nineteenth century. He adds that 'its graduates, as a whole, contributed relatively little to the development of pure and applied science. Indeed, between 1804 and 1880, an orientation towards the *Ecole polytechnique* constituted above all a kind of legitimization for the ruling class'[8].

Had this legitimization function been foreseen or desired by the founders of the establishment or the original legislators? At all events, a law of 1799 reorganizing the *Ecole polytechnique* gives no reason to think so, since it states that the purpose of the institution is to train students for the vocational schools of the public services and learned men to spread scientific knowledge throughout the country[9]. Many *polytechniciens* did in fact carry out this second function by organizing courses in provincial offshoots of the *Conservatoire des arts et métiers* and also, in 1830, by establishing the *Association polytechnique*, which was the first instrument of popular education.

Could it be that the drifting away of the *Ecole polytechnique* from its original functions was made possible by the existence of other interests and motivations in the minds of the founders? In his preface to Shinn's book, Furet speaks of a 'law of peripheral development' of higher education, by which he means that 'in order to respond to the spirit of the age, the central authorities created new institutions . . . specializing in new disciplines or those which have taken on a new lease of life . . ., complementary to and in competition with the university'.

Among these new institutions were the *Collège de France*, the military schools and the engineering schools. One might think that this desire to respond to 'the spirit of the age' contributed both to reinforcing the selective nature of the institution and to turning out individuals capable of adapting themselves to different functions. This selectiveness pervaded higher technical education as a whole, where different kinds of establishment catered for different clienteles and different functions.

At the top of the pyramid, the *Ecole polytechnique* produced the engineers of the national administration, whose double function, both technical and administrative, attracted the upper-middle classes. Subsequently, the *Ecole centrale des arts et manufactures*, founded in 1829, provided for the needs of industrialization. This establishment recruited primarily from the intermediate ranks of the middle classes. Finally, newer schools such as the *Ecole supérieure de physique et de chimie* and the *Ecole supérieure d'électricité*, which were founded from 1880 on, sought their students more among the lower-middle classes, with a more specialized training[10].

Thus, in the very process of building up the system of higher technical education, we can see at work the élitist and intellectualizing trend, giving priority and preponderance to general education, which characterized the construction of the entire system.

2. *The middle level*

During the course of the nineteenth century, the progress of industrialization brought about a need for a core of factory 'non-commissioned officers' able to act as intermediaries between higher management and the workers.

To respond to this need, different formulae were conceived and tried out, for example the higher primary schools of Guizot and the special education proposed by Duruy. However, it was not until the war of 1870 and the Paris Communes had provided matter for reflection and driven home various ideas that an attempt was made to set up a proper network of technical schools with the object of training foremen and junior managers. Among others, we may mention the technical schools of the city of Paris, such as the *Ecole Diderot*, founded in 1873, and the national vocational schools which began in 1881.

In his book on the *Ecole Diderot*, Y. Legoux shows that this establishment fulfilled other functions than that of training technicians capable of being both specialists and organization men. In effect, the *Ecole Diderot* represented both a springboard for the promotion of many sons of manual workers and a net to catch children of higher social classes who had not followed the educational channels traditional for people of their background[11].

3. *The elementary level*

The steps taken to develop elementary technical education spring from the same technical and social considerations. As an illustration of this, let us look at the Astier law which, in 1919, provided for the institution of vocational courses for apprentices during working hours, and later, in 1944, of apprenticeship centres.

The Astier law represented one of the side-effects of a persistent nineteenth-century urge to control youth through various forms of post-scholastic teaching and popular education. Immediately following the First World War, the needs of reconstruction added an economic motivation to the social one.

As to the apprenticeship centres, though no doubt in a new spirit, they were simply a continuation of the vocational training centres created in 1939 to meet the needs of the war and subsequently multiplied by the Vichy Government to provide a framework for the youth of the country.

In both cases, it appears difficult to distinguish the social from the economic function of elementary technical education.

In the course of recent decades, the transformation of the apprenticeship centres into colleges of technical education (1960) and then into vocational *lycées* (1977) illustrates the second tendency in the evolution of the system of technical education.

Second trend: an upward movement

The process of construction from the top down was accompanied by a second movement, already illustrated by the evolution of adult education, which led establishments originally intended to provide elementary instruction to working-class children to become socially selective and provide a higher level of education.

In some cases the elementary programmes served as a model for the higher levels. Thus, for example, the revolutionary courses for armaments workers organized in 1794 (*l'An II*) in order to promote the spread of technical, pedagogical and patriotic education, found an echo in other sectors of social life, notably the creation and organization of the *Ecole normale supérieure* the following year. In other cases, the structures, functions and recruitment of various establishments were profoundly affected. Thus, the first schools of arts and crafts, set up right at the beginning of the nineteenth century for the training of workers and foremen, gradually changed into engineering schools. In the same way, the *Conservatoire des arts et métiers*, founded in 1794 as a sort of technical museum open to the public at large, changed in 1819 to 'a *haute école* for the application of science to commerce and industry'[12].

In the transition from a lower to a higher level, a branch of education is subject to both separation and integration. On the one hand, the function of technical training tends to separate it from others to which it was formerly closely linked such as, for example, the teaching of the rudiments of knowledge, military training and production assistance. On the other hand, it becomes integrated into the education system as a whole, either as a result of administrative rearrangements or by the reorganization of programmes and a higher proportion of the timetable reserved for general education. The two processes occur simultaneously while nevertheless adapting themselves to the evolution of professional structures. Thus, while the amount of time allocated to general education may increase in some programmes, it may at the same time decrease in others.

In certain historical situations, the function of social segregation fulfilled by technical education may prevail over its economic function. To take an example, let us consider the place and role of the teaching of draughtsmanship in the central schools of the Revolution. Attached as they were to the empirical-sensualist tradition, the founders of these establishments took this subject as the basis of a programme of secondary education. However, for students of modest origins, these courses acquired above all a vocational or pre-vocational significance, so that they enrolled for them in large numbers. One of the officials responsible for the central schools, Destutt de Tracy, found this state of affairs intolerable and stated in no uncertain terms their non-professional nature[13]:

'We have two complete systems of public education,' he declared on 5 February 1800 to the *Conseil d'instruction publique*. 'For the working classes there are the primary schools and apprenticeships to different trades. For the educated classes there are the central and specialized schools. I do not advise giving the latter to a child destined to become an artisan any more than I recommend giving the former to one likely to become a statesman or man of letters.'

Two years later the substitution of *lycées* for the central schools appeared to confirm the views of Destutt de Tracy inasmuch as it brought about both a far-reaching change in the academic programmes and more rigorous selection. Thus the function of social differentiation turned out to be more important than the academic interests of the founders of the central schools.

In this connection, let us remember that the age-old prejudices with respect to elementary technical education appear to relate less to engineering or technology itself than to a well-established confusion between these activities, the social status and the psychological characteristics attributed to those who exercise them, and the corresponding educational institutions.

It should be added that situations and behaviour varied considerably from one country to another. In nineteenth-century England the profession of engineer, being considered a sort of ladder for young people from the working class, enjoyed a lower social status than in Germany or the United States. Moreover, having been the first to industrialize, by the end of the nineteenth century the English were prisoners of attitudes and ideas formed at a time when practical skills played a predominant role in the evolution of technology. G. Roderick and M. Stephens attribute some weight to these two factors in seeking to explain the backwardness of the United Kingdom compared with these other two countries at the time when what is known as 'the second industrial revolution' (involving the use of oil and electricity) created a need for better general and technical qualifications[14].

Thus the history of technical education cannot be reduced to the interplay of simple and unilateral determinisms. Bound up with social, political and psychological evolution, the progress of technology and changes affecting professional structures are not in themselves enough to account for the functions really carried out by vocational training establishments. This being so, what is the real significance of the resounding statements and campaigns which recur from time to time concerning the rehabilitation of technical education or manual labour?

Technological culture in our time

In spite of changes and improvements in the organization and working of technical education, psychologists and educators continue to be faced with the same problems: why is an orientation towards primary technical schools so often considered as a sign of failure? Within these schools, why is it so difficult to co-ordinate a general and a practical education? Why do so many drop out in the course of their training? And nowadays, why cannot the technological revolution, the mutation of professional structures, the intellectualization of work and the growth of the tertiary sector provide us with a solution to these problems? In more general terms, is not the very notion of technical education called into question by the amalgamation of what J. Habermas calls 'a complex whole consisting of science, engineering, the armed forces and the administration'?

In this connection, technical education is currently undergoing a double process of integration. First, we see an integration with the education system as a whole: for example, does an initiation in electronics and computer science belong to general or to vocational education? Second, one may observe an integration with the world of work: various formulae for continuing or alternating education divide the task of teaching between the school and the company.

Faced with this situation, which is both complex and difficult to grasp, one may ask which way research should turn.

Over and above the restrictive use of history, which tends to reduce current problems to a simple matter of age-old prejudices, there is room for real historical research which would consist, on the one hand, of going more deeply into the upward and downward movements characteristic of the evolution of institutions and, on the other, of defining the functions performed by technical education according to the different kinds of establishment. Historical enquiry finds its 'natural' continuation in sociological studies on the circumstances of contemporary institutional development and on the effects of technical education.

Analysis of these effects is also a field for research in educational psychology. Among other things, such research is naturally concerned with a number of subjects in its own field. In particular, this is true of the study of the complex relationships between general and vocational education at different levels and in the different sectors of technical education. Such a study relates not only to the industrialized countries, but also to newly founded countries where the phenomenon of rejection of technical education stems partly from the colonial heritage. In addition, research in educational psychology can help to discredit a certain summary psychology which limits its goals to the classification of individuals by reference to a dubious typology (for example, practical or abstract disposition) and which, by the same token, hides the social functions of technical education. Instead of limiting itself to measuring and then classifying behaviour, the true educational psychology of technical education should, for example, investigate how and under what influences – family, school or the media – the attitudes and images of children and adolescents towards technology are formed; and how, in such conditions, and thanks to what teaching methods, mastery of a technological subject is attained.

In view of the new relations which are being formed between education and employment, one might envisage replacing technical education by a technological education with a view to better adaptation to the requirements of the modern world, based on a better grasp of its main characteristics. If this were done, manual work would tend to become one of the elements of general and multidimensional education which every young person would receive.

In this case, what would become of technical culture? This is not the place to go into the definitions commonly given of various types of culture, for example literary, scientific, technical, formal and so on. Let us simply note that with the constant enlargement of the cultural field, particularly in the case of historical research, it is difficult to think of anything which does not come under the heading of culture! It should also be pointed out that cultural problems can only be analysed by a comparative approach. Thus, according to W. Hörner, the distinction – one might even speak of the opposition – which exists between literary and scientific culture in France is much less marked in the Federal Republic of Germany, where an effort is made to synthesize the two cultures[15].

Within the framework of a single country, the comparison of two supposedly antagonistic and unalterable cultures (for example, literary and technical or élite and popular, etc.) is often based on a double confusion: first, between objects of culture and cultural behaviour; and second, between private or subjective values such as religion or art and universal ones such as science and, to a large extent, technology. While it would seem difficult to establish any order of rank between objects of culture in different fields (for example, as between a piece of music, a technical instrument or product, or a sporting event) it is nevertheless possible, in each of these fields, to distinguish various forms and perhaps even levels of cultural behaviour. In view of these distinctions, a cultural education would be designed, on the one hand, to enable the individual to acquire more insight and exploit all the resources of a given cultural object; and, on the other, to encourage him to enlarge his cultural horizon, to pass on from one object to others in other fields[16].

With the help of these preliminary remarks, we can now go on to cast more light on the notion of technical culture.

In the first place we should be clear that, like any other cultural object, an object of technology is multi-faceted. It can be approached from historical, scientific, economic, aesthetic or other angles. From a historical point of view, for example, according to B. Köpeczi, the interest will lie less in studying successive manufacturing processes of tools or products than in analysing 'the influence of material culture, the uses which are made of tools and products, their relation to working conditions, and the nature of the work'[17].

These facets, then, derive both from subjective or personal values (as in the case of aesthetic aspects) and from universal ones relating to accumulated knowledge (in the case of scientific aspects). Cultural behaviour would consist of exploring all the different facets of an object of technology, on the one hand, and, on the other, of the result of this exploration, proceeding to seek out other cultural objects. The study of such transfer phenomena belongs to the educational psychology approach to cultural problems.

However, in order fully to play its part as a cultural object, in other words to serve as a base for exploration, deeper investigation and transfer, a technological object must be recognized and as it were legitimized by 'authorities' more or less remote from the world of technology itself.

In this connection, as we have had occasion to emphasize, the generally reserved and critical attitude to technology and technical education stems not only from long-standing prejudice and the confusion between an activity, those who carry it out and the institutions which teach it. It also arises from certain overall ideas regarding the relationship between human beings and technology.

We are all aware of the pessimistic view voiced long ago by Spengler when he foresaw the collapse of what he called 'Faustian culture', in other words a culture characterized by the triumph of technological thought:

Our eye for history, our faculty of writing history, is a revealing sign that our path lies downward. At the peaks of the high Cultures, just as they are passing over into Civilizations, this gift of penetrating recognition comes to them for a moment, and only for a moment. [. . .] The lord of the World is becoming the slave of the Machine, which is forcing him – forcing us all, whether we are aware of it or not – to follow its course. The victor, crashed, is dragged to death by the team[18].

The present crisis, associated with the rapid burgeoning of 'techno-science', tends to support the pessimistic point of view. Referring to genetic engineering, the philosopher G. Hottois confronts technology with ethics. In his opinion, 'the philosophical and collective conscience tolerates only symbolic manipulation of the human, usually in some way relating to language, as for example in education, acculturation, propaganda, or the influence of ideologies or the media'. Whereas the symbolic manipulations belong to 'the natural cultural essence of man', technological intervention is foreign to this essence. Thus, the philosopher should 'spontaneously take the side of ethics, assimilating the other tendency to absolute evil, mainly the blind, dumb temptation to escape from the field of ethics and, by the same token, from all that speaks of the essence of man'[19].

More subtly, in his essay entitled *La technique et la science comme idéolo-gie*[20], J. Habermas readdresses a long-disputed theme: is intelligence a child of technology or of the city, of acting on things or of acting on human beings? He distinguishes two forms of rationality. On the one hand, at a scientific and technological level, work represents a rational activity relating to a goal. On the other, from the institutional point of view, we have inter-action, communication via the medium of language. After examining these alternatives, Habermas favours a balance between *homo faber* and *homo loquax*, while expressing a fear that science and technology may take the place of traditional forms of legitimization of power and domination:

To the exact extent to which science and technology infiltrate the institutions of society, thus transforming them, the ancient modes of legitimization are destroyed. The secularization and removing from their pedestal of those images of the world which orient human action, and indeed the whole cultural tradition, are the corollary of an increasingly 'rational' social acti-vity[21].

Is the science of history in a position to decide or, at least, to contribute usefully to this debate? No doubt it enables us to keep the present crisis in proportion by recalling the cyclical nature of human beings' relations with technology. In addition, the historian can throw a favourable light on scien-tific and technical progress by stressing its beneficial consequences. He may even go so far as to question the idea that human nature is unchangeable. But in doing so, may he not run a risk of exceeding his role as research worker and teacher?

What then are the functions of history and the responsibilities of the his-torian?

NOTES AND REFERENCES

1. Deforge, Y. *Le graphisme technique: son histoire et son enseignement.* Seyssel, France, Champ Vallon, 1981. 256 p.
2. Léon, A. *Formation générale et apprentissage du métier.* Paris, Presses universitaires de France, 1965. 400 p.
3. Ibid.
4. Ward, L.O. Technical education and the politicians (1870–1918). *British journal of educa-tional studies* (Oxford, United Kingdom), Vol. XXI, no. 1, February, 1973, p. 34–39.
5. Léon, A. *La révolution française et l'éducation technique.* Paris, Centre national de la re-cherche scientifique, Société des Etudes robespierristes, 1968. 313 p.
6. Bouvier-Ajam, M. *Essai de méthodologie historique.* Paris, Ed. Le Pavillon, 1971. 104 p.
7. Léon, A. *La révolution française et l'éducation technique.* Op. cit.
8. Shinn, T. *Savoir scientifique et pouvoir social: l'Ecole polytechnique (1794–1914).* Paris, Presses de la Fondation nationale des sciences politiques, 1980. 272 p.
9. Léon, A. *La révolution française et l'éducation technique.* Op. cit.
10. Thépot, A. Les institutions scientifiques et techniques au XIXe siècle. *Histoire de l'éducation* (Paris, Institut national de recherche pédagogique), no. 18, avril 1983, p. 83–95.

11. Legoux, Y. *Du compagnon au technicien: l'École Diderot et l'évolution des qualifications.* Paris, Technique et Vulgarisation, 1972.

12. Léon, A. *La révolution française et l'éducation technique.* Op. cit.

13. Ibid.

14. Roderick, G.W.; Stephens, M. Education and training for English engineers in the late nineteenth and early twentieth century. *Annals of science* (Basingstoke, United Kingdom), no. 2, 1971, p. 143–163.

15. Hörner, W. L'évolution de la notion de culture dans la discussion pédagogique française. *Paedagogica historica* (Ghent, Belgium), vol. XVIII, no. 2, 1978, p. 342–355.

16. Léon, A. *Histoire de l'éducation populaire en France.* Paris, Nathan, 1983.

17. Köpeczi, B. Objet et méthode de l'histoire de la culture. *La pensée* (Paris, Institut de recherches marxistes), no. 200, 1978, p. 21–32.

18. Spengler, O. *Man and technics: a contribution to a philosophy of life.* Westport, CT, Greenwood Press, 1976, p. 14, 90–91.

19. Hottois, G. Ethique et technique. *Bulletin de la Société française de philosophie* (Paris), no. 3, 1982, p. 79–97.

20. Habermas, J. *La technique et la science comme idéologie.* Paris, Gonthier, 1978. 272 p.

21. Ibid.

PART THREE

The functions of
the history of education

CHAPTER VIII

The interest in
and uses of history

It is possible to adopt different approaches to the question of the functions of history, the scope to be accorded to it in teaching, or the requirements which it is supposed to satisfy.

One may attach prior importance to the interest expressed by children and adults in history either as a subject for teaching or for cultural diffusion or amusement, as in radio programmes, historical novels and comic strips. Historians, who themselves form part of the public, have their own motivations with regard to historical research.

The degree of interest displayed in history does not necessarily coincide with its usefulness or its functions in the eyes of historians, teachers or the public at large.

The functions attributed to history as taught or widely diffused are always of a relative, hypothetical nature. This applies to the short- or long-term effects of any academic discipline or education. Thus the various points of view expressed concerning the functions of history call for research (evaluation and transfer process) relating partly to experimental teaching. Whether oriented towards the interest or the usefulness of history, such research can only be undertaken after finding answers to the following questions:

1. What kind of history are we talking about? Do we mean historical narrative or the investigation of particular problem areas? Are we interested in the history of scholastic institutions or in that of teaching techniques? (At this point we may refer to the distinctions drawn in Chapters II and III.)

In this connection, the distinction drawn between narrative and problem history is associated with other pairs relating to the functions of history, the methods of the historian and the activity of the teacher all at the same time. The following pairs summarize some contemporary controversies regarding history and the teaching of history: chronological history/

thematic history; event-oriented history/long-term history; mythological use of the past/
critical and multidimensional analysis of the past; the political or civic function of history/the
intellectual or affective function of history; ideological teachers/motivating teachers. These
pairs combine with the various modes of historical culture, for example scientific, curricular
or extra-curricular. The ensuing contradictions set the teacher difficult problems of choice
and synthesis.

2. What public is envisaged? Are we thinking of professional historians, student historians, educators (for example teachers, administrators or
   parents) or pupils? Should the general public, whose interest in history is
   proved by the success of various radio and television programmes, also be
   kept in mind?
3. What effects is it proposed to study? Is the object to investigate immediate
   effects of the teaching of history, such as intellectual and affective education, or longer-term ones, such as occupations chosen or social and political action? Is there also an interest in such teaching at school level with
   respect to cultural behaviour?
4. What period is to be taken into account?

Regarding this last question, it should be remembered that the interest in
history and the decision to study historiography are also historically determined. In other words, change, whether perceived, hoped for or feared, and
the resulting view of the future, whether encouraging or sombre, influence
people's attitudes both to history and to the past. Thus, according to Ariès[1],
the present popularity of history is related to a diminished faith in progress
and to a preference for the preservation of cultural traditions rather than
modernity. 'As a fantasy,' he writes, 'the enthusiasm for history may take the
place of reality and politics.' For his part, Veyne associates the interest in
history with a need for self-knowledge, itself linked to a weakening of the
will to affirmation or power[2].

The foregoing comment shows the closeness of the links which, via the
study of motivations and functions, bind together historiography, the teaching of history and its popularization.

This chapter is concerned only with the motivations of historical research
and with ways of presenting the usefulness of history to students of educational history. The next chapter will deal both with the general functions of
history and with the difficulties of teaching it as a subject. In view of the
small number of research projects explicitly concerned with the functions of
the history of education, most of the information and discussion in Part
Three will relate to general history. However, while the arguments concerning
the interest or usefulness of history may be valid for all branches of the
subject, it is reasonable to think that reference to the educational problems
of the past may help to strengthen the historical motivation of the various
partners in the educational process.

The motivation of historical research

From ancient times, the motivations of the historian have been divided between the desire to arrive at the truth and that of advising men of action. In this connection, one may contrast the 'committed' history of Polybius with the 'neutral' history of Thucydides or, more generally, the purpose of Plato with that of Aristotle: 'Plato wrote *The Republic* with a view to the improvement of city states, whereas Aristotle wrote his *Politics* in order to develop a better theory'[3].

From the Renaissance on, the multiplication of well-paid and influential royal historiographers, together with the creation of numerous chairs of history in different European countries, helped to affirm the practical and political functions of history[4]. However, the desire for accuracy and other more personal interests continued to motivate historians in their work.

A primary motivation, common to both the specialist and the non-specialist, is the sheer interest of evoking the past. 'Even if history were unable to render any other services,' writes M. Bloch in this connection, 'it would still have to be admitted that it is absorbing . . . because the review of human activities, with which it is primarily concerned, is of all subjects the one most calculated to inspire the imagination'[5]. The investigation or contemplation of such a spectacle satisfies a curiosity 'the justification of which is as much human as theoretical, existential and not purely intellectual'[6].

This curiosity is itself historically conditioned. Its aims and underlying psychological structures vary from one period to another. According to F. Chatelet, a truly historical outlook was not able to develop until profane, chronological time took the place of 'sacred', indefinitely recoverable time, and also of the temporal heterogeneity implicit in the great epics[7]. This substitution worked in favour of political mutations: 'the cultural decision to write history stems from man's awareness of the political dimension of his destiny, his consciousness of being an agent in this physical, profane world and in the midst of a community on which he depends, in other words understanding of the nature of real liberty'[8]. In short, narrative man is first and foremost one who becomes aware of himself as the cause. This theory, whereby the first category of historical consciousness is the state of waiting or of formulating a plan, springs from analysis of the evolution of Greek thought in the fifth century B.C. It relates more particularly to the works of Herodotus and of Thucydides and to the meaning of the Persian and Peloponnesian Wars. But it also throws new light on other periods of history. Thus, at the beginning of the Third Republic in France, the proliferation of books on the history of education would seem to be connected with the perspectives opened up by the institution of mass elementary education. Nearer to our own time, the number of works on the past of Third World countries would appear to be the result of the interplay of similar forces.

It could be that the attempt to bring the past back to life represents a need to escape, a reluctance to confront the difficulties of the real world, a 'morbid' curiosity, a desire to imagine oneself different from what one is[9]. It is to be noted, as Veyne puts it, that 'the theatre of history arouses passions in the spectator which, being experienced at an intellectual level, undergo a kind of purification; their gratuitousness renders vain any sentiment which is not apolitical'[10].

However, emotional motivations, and in particular the need to find certainties in the past, are in no way foreign to the reasons for undertaking historical research. Indeed, such research gives the individual 'the awareness of belonging to a totality which transcends him' and enables him to 'rise above the individualistic self'[11]. Let us add that the desire to refer to the past is strengthened by the feeling of isolation in the present. At the beginning of the last century, the founders of the mutual schools replied to their critics by pointing to the example of the Hebrews and the Jesuits, or by quoting Erasmus and Rollin. Less than thirty years ago, the defenders of programmed teaching gladly referred to Socrates, Quintilian or Descartes[12].

Whatever the nature of the motivations which orient historians, they cannot evade the responsibility arising from the popularization of their work and the uses to which it is put.

The responsibilities of the historian

At first sight, these responsibilities would appear to be limited by the epistemological status of history. In effect, free of all control, of any practical sanction, the speculative craft of the historian would appear to justify Paul Valéry's jibe: 'The historian does for the past what the fortune-teller does for the future. But unlike the historian, she is subject to verification'[13].

Nevertheless, the historian, like the fortune-teller, is led willy-nilly to exercise a more or less profound influence on the representation of the attitudes and actions of his contemporaries. Attention is sometimes drawn to the demiurgic role of the historian who, in the course of his work, holds up to public admiration or reprobation some forgotten or little-known personality. Certain specialists believe that this influence is exerted via the development of a collective consciousness. For them, history is at the same time the science and the consciousness of movement, the dawning of collective awareness facilitating such movement: 'The history of a collective awareness, the initiation of movement by this awareness, the collective judgement of such movement as progress, seem to us to be, among other things, three major characteristics and perhaps three glories of human history'[14].

Even if the historian abjures any desire to influence the behaviour of his contemporaries, the ambiguity of his task, which was analysed in Part One

The uses of history   95

of the present work, affects his relationship to both knowledge and action.
De Paepe distinguishes four aspects of this ambiguity[15]:
— For the historian, the fact that history is rooted in the present constitutes
  both a stimulus and a source of error.
— His interest in general trends may lead him to conceal or underestimate
  the particularities of a situation or a period.
— The desire for objectivity in collecting, filtering and interpreting historical
  data may compromise his commitment or hinder critical intervention in
  the cultural and political field.
— Insofar as it derives both from the science of history and that of pedagogics, the history of education is subject to tensions which manifest themselves in the difficulties experienced by the research worker when called
  upon to satisfy both the requirements of historiography and the expectations of educators.
With regard to these expectations, A. Momigliano considers that the requirements of teaching maintain or increase the tendency to draw hasty or
insufficiently documented conclusions. 'Since the principles of religion,
philosophy and morals have lost their authority,' he adds, 'there has grown
up a custom of asking the historian either for a religious or moral interpretation
of the past or for a precise forecast of the future'[16].

   This drift in the role of historiography is bound to increase with the growing popular demand for history and its ever-prominent place in the media.
Other historians consider that the requirements of teaching and popular
demand represent stimuli indispensable to the development of historical research. Since we are not in a position to decide the outcome of this important
debate, let us consult some teachers (who are also students in educational
science) about their view of the usefulness of history.

The usefulness of educational history as seen by a group of teachers

In 1982–83 thirty-two students following a *maîtrise* course at the University
of Paris V on the history of education, most of whom were primary or secondary school-teachers, were asked to reply to the following open question:
'What use is the history of education?' Their replies mainly related to knowledge and, in certain cases, to the relation between knowledge and action.

   From a cognitive point of view, the supposed contributions of history took
place at different levels. They ranged from a knowledge of the evolution of
educational institutions via the study of processes, factors and mechanisms,
to philosophical interrogation. More precisely, the answers can be grouped
under five main headings:

Generalizations, sometimes vague. This group simply affirmed the utility of knowing about past education systems, and the evolution of ideas, institutions and practices.

The present is the result of evolution. The idea here is that the history of education represents a framework of reference necessary to the understanding of present-day educational situations.

The study of processes, mechanisms and factors. Here the accent is on picking out permanent and changing factors, phenomena of persistence and points of rupture. There is an interest in relations between various historical theories (for example, socio-economic variables and the movement of ideas) and, thanks to the history of education, it is hoped to reach a better understanding of general history. The historical interest is sometimes focused on the way in which society ensures its continuity, thus relating to certain philosophical concerns.

Philosophical interrogation. Here we are concerned not only with asking questions about the relationships between the past, the present and the future, but also in trying to understand what we have now become. In this connection, history is seen as being able to give a sense of direction to human destiny. Questions also arise on whether a knowledge of history has played a motivating or inhibiting role in the evolution of humanity.

Knowledge and action. Some replies related rather to preparing for action: playing down the significance of modern innovations and theories; displaying a critical state of mind; understanding the interactions between individuals, groups and society, in order to envisage possibilities of intervention; and becoming aware of one's responsibilities as a citizen. Other replies dealt more directly with methods of action, with the use of 'schools' of history, the search for answers to present-day problems, the avoidance of past mistakes; in brief, to weigh up the advantages and disadvantages of former educational practices with a view to learning lessons for the present and the future.

Two remarks are called for in presenting these few results of a limited enquiry. In the first place, with regard to the contribution of history to personal development, cognitive aspects are considered more important – or at least are more explicitly discussed – than affective aspects. Should we recognize in this the very spirit of French university education? Second, with regard to the practical scope of historical knowledge, we should note the distinction between the replies dealing with the preparation for action and those which directly concerned action itself. These two remarks will be the starting-point for a more thorough analysis of the functions of the history of education.

NOTES AND REFERENCES

1. Ariès, P., et al. La nouvelle histoire. *Magazine littéraire* (Paris), no. 123, p. 10–23.
2. Ibid.
3. Veyne, P. *Comment on écrit l'historie.* Paris, Seuil, 1971. 352 p.
4. Chatelet, F. *La naissance de l'histoire.* Paris, Minuit, 1962.
5. Bloch, M. *Apologie pour l'histoire au métier d'historien.* 4th ed. Paris, Colin, 1961.
6. Aron, R. *Introduction à la philosophie de l'histoire. Essai sur les limites de l'objectivité historique.* 2nd ed. Paris, Gallimard, 1948.
7. Chatelet, F. *Op. cit.*
8. Ibid.
9. Marrou, H.-I. *De la connaissance historique.* 4th ed. Paris, Seuil, 1962.
10. Veyne, P. *Op. cit.*
11. Goldmann, L. *Sciences humaines et philosophie.* Paris, Presses universitaires de France, 1952.
12. Léon, A. Investigation psychologique et recherche historique. *Bulletin de psychologie* (Groupe d'études de psychologie, Université de Paris), vol. 18, no. 7–9, 1964, p. 351–358.
13. Valéry, P. *Regards sur le monde actuel.* Paris, Stock, 1931.
14. Labrousse, E. Structure sociale et histoire. *Raison présente* (Paris), no. 7, 1968, p. 41–72.
15. De Paepe, J.-L. *La valeur de l'histoire de l'éducation par rapport aux politiques éducatives: Quelques réflexions méthodologiques.* 21 p. (Paper presented at the third symposium of the International Association for the History of Education, Sèvres, 1981.)
16. Momigliano, A. L'histoire à l'âge des idéologies. *Le débat* (Paris), no. 23, 1983, p. 129–146.

CHAPTER IX

Attitudes to historical knowledge

The functions which history fulfils by means of research, teaching and cultural diffusion relate to different aspects of the existence of individuals and communities. The preceding chapter dealt mainly with the motivations and responsibilities of the historian. This time, we shall be mainly, though not exclusively, concerned with the 'consumers' of history.

No doubt the various effects which history is supposed to have form a whole, but for the sake of clarity we will classify them here into three groups. The first group contains the effects relating to development of the individual personality from an intellectual, affective, moral or social point of view. The second, more specifically concerned with the history of education, relates to the role of this discipline in the analysis of present-day pedagogical situations. Finally, it will be well to consider how far history can serve as a guide for action.

Before going on to discuss the scope of these effects, we should keep in mind that the study of the relationship of human beings to historical knowledge is much more in the nature of an exchange or confrontation of points of view than of research as such.

A means of personal development

It would be easy enough to list the main 'virtues' with which historical education is commonly credited. While satisfying our legitimate curiosity about the past, such an education is supposed to exercise the imagination, develop our critical faculties and our sense of relativity, to broaden our temporal horizon, and so on.

To take an example, let us consider the development of critical awareness. Inasmuch as historical enquiry, through the exploitation of numerous and varied sources, enables us to pierce smoke-screens and refute false information regarding some event in the past, it may prompt the individual to a more vigilant attitude to the rumours or false propaganda which are not lacking in the modern world.

At the affective level, history seems to satisfy the need for coherence, continuity, solidarity and roots in the past. Satisfaction of these needs goes together with awareness of a tradition or the assuming of a heritage which it is desired to maintain or enrich. In this connection we need only think of the place which the ideas and achievements of the past occupied in the minds of the pioneers of the 'new' education. In addition, the process of identification with the great educators of the past tends to arouse respect for their work and humility on the part of their present successors[1].

History can also help to preserve or increase the spirit of tolerance in that the process of distinguishing different levels in the analysis of the past and various orders of factors in the determination of events prohibits hasty or one-sided judgement of groups or individuals, encouraging us rather to place ideas or actions in their context.

Finally, there is no need to recall the fact that, over and above the world of education, the teaching of history is considered as a factor of social and national cohesion. In this connection C.O. Carbonell has written: 'No group is amnesiac. To remember is for it to exist; to forget is to disappear.' To the instinctive memory of the animal, humanity adds 'cultural memory, the only kind capable of exorcizing death and founding the heritage of knowledge'[2]. Nevertheless, it should be stressed that several 'cultural' memories may coexist peacefully or in hostility within the borders of a single country.

This brief review of the main possible effects of history on personal development and on the constitution of a collective consciousness calls for two comments.

The first refers to the distinction drawn in Chapter III between 'narrative' and 'problem' history. It relates to the place of national history relative to these two historiographical orientations. More precisely, is it possible to exalt and build up national unity without selecting and giving particular importance to certain events or personalities and without at the same time giving preference to the narrative approach? In this respect, a professor of history has noted that the sense of national identity and the collective memory are cultivated in particular by usages and customs, and that this was the case long before mass education appeared during the nineteenth century. He adds that, paradoxically, 'the only period when the collective memory was strengthened by the school (but also by the press and the army) was at the end of the nineteenth and the beginning of the twentieth centuries, both in France and in the German Empire; and this led to one of the most gigantic slaughters in the history of humanity'[3]. In other words, in the course of fulfilling its various functions, does not history run some risk of a dichotomy between critical intelligence and the urge to respond to certain affective and social requirements? We shall return to this question when dealing with the contents of school history books.

The second comment relates to the specific nature of the effects ascribed to the study of history. 'One's judgement on a history book,' writes B. Croce, 'cannot be based on the degree to which it stirs the imagination, on the emotion and emulation which it excites, or on the extent to which it arouses curiosity or helps to pass the time. Such effects can equally well be obtained by fiction and drama'[4]. Such a statement sends us back to the difficult problem of evaluating the cultural importance of any discipline or any educational action. Does this importance depend primarily on content, on form or on method?

Further ambiguities appear when we examine the extent to which history enables us to analyse current educational situations.

An analytical tool for contemporary situations

Any reflection on the present time, any attempt to analyse a current educational situation, implies some reference to the past. In effect, such a reflection or attempt refers us to some picture of the past either experienced (in the sense of one's own experience as a pupil) or conceived (as a result of the instruction in history received at school).

The weight of the past or the light cast on contemporary situations by the study of the past may be estimated in different ways.

In the first place, existing institutions, as for example the geographical distribution of schools, represent a transient combination where one may discern at the same time the survival of older networks of establishments and the emergence of new ones. Any country which has achieved independence in the course of recent decades can supply many examples of the motley nature of its school distribution map.

Second, inasmuch as tradition always counts for a good deal in the plans or decisions of politicians, reference to the past makes it possible to identify which of the proposed reforms really contain anything new[5].

Consciously or not, tradition also reflects the attitudes and present images of educators and users of the education system. In Chapter VII we have already had occasion to mention the long-standing prejudices against technical education. One might also cite the way in which evening courses continue to follow the lines laid down in the nineteenth century, according to the picture which adults and young people had formed of continuing education at a time when it was first becoming general.

The study of the phenomenon of persistence is sometimes enriched by the results of comparative or differential research into, for example, the opinion of parents from different social categories regarding the functions of the nursery school, including education, instruction and care of children. The most frequent conclusion of this type of research is that new ideas begin at the most cultivated level and spread downwards.

However, there remains a problem of a genuinely psychological kind regarding the way in which, throughout history, attitudes and views which have grown up in the past outlive their time. Authors who have investigated this problem have tentatively posited the notion of the collective subconscious or that of a cognitive framework preceding any process of formal learning or memorization. It goes without saying that family upbringing, schooling and the alternative school play a major role in such persistence phenomena[6].

The study of existing situations may take into account the 'tendential laws' which express the existence of certain regularities in the working of institutions. These laws have already been mentioned in Chapter VII in connection with the history of technical education. One might consider some other recurrent phenomena as side-effects of the intellectualist and élitist tradition, or that of the system of streaming.

The application of history to analysis of the present carries with it a certain risk of projecting present-day values and structures on to the past, and also of recruiting the past in defence of modern causes. Nevertheless, without underestimating the importance of these phenomena in juxtaposing the past and the present, it may be considered that history can throw light on possible courses of action.

A guide for action

How important are the tendential laws which we can derive from the historical study of some institution?

Let us begin by saying that such laws are not forecasting instruments. However much pressure the past may exert on the present, any educational situation is, at a given time, the result of numerous economic, political and cultural influences whose interplay is far from being perfectly understood. Moreover, the accelerating pace of change which nowadays affects the conditions, forms and results of educational action make it impossible to extrapolate from slower or less complicated trends. To be convinced of the truth of this statement, it is only necessary to remember the outcome of many forecasts drawn up shortly before the present crisis began.

History must thus constantly assume the contradiction between, on the one hand, offering ever more subtle and pertinent analyses and explanations, and, on the other, refusing any kind of forecast. The duty of the historian, according to R. Storr, is indeed to enlighten the public with regard to what his speciality has led him to observe, namely 'the tendency of Americans to turn to education in times of crisis'. However, he adds, the aim of history is not to impose some acceptable doctrine but to draw attention to new problems[7].

In examining the possibilities, however modest, which knowledge may offer for the improvement of present practices, we shall return to the distinction drawn in Chapter VIII between preparation for action and action as such.

Regarding the direct influence of the 'lessons' of history, we may think of the adaptation of practices which had some success in the past and which appear to be potentially effective again in similar circumstances. A notable example of this was the application in Third World countries of basic educational methods developed in Western countries during the nineteenth century. We have already had occasion in Chapter VI to mention the failures and the complexity of the problems occasioned by this transfer.

Former practices can be the subject of critical analysis aimed at identifying mistakes to be avoided in future or to keep educational fashions in perspective. Think, for example, of the hopes and passions aroused by the changing phases of attractive teaching or by the various applications of the 'demultiplication' model of education. Another instance of direct utilization of the teachings of the past is militant action; the desire to be, here and now, an agent of history, an inheritor and propagator of the work accomplished by revered elders.

Leaving action behind us and proceeding now to preparation for action, we can draw a distinction between motivational, stimulative attitudes to historical knowledge, such as identification with some group or the recognition of roots in the past, and inhibiting, regulatory, cognitive attitudes such as the sense of proportion and the preservation of an alert critical faculty. With regard to the first group, one might say that in so far as it reveals the extent of change in the education system under the influence of various factors, history is apt to stimulate present action; and in fact, it would be enough to understand these factors thoroughly and direct them to the requirements of some educational project.

With respect to the inhibiting or regulatory aspects, the abiding gap between what is said and what is actually achieved incites us to adopt a careful or even a critical attitude to any educational treatise. Furthermore, inasmuch as it stresses the element of doubt concerning the outcome of any innovation or decision, pointing to the importance and frequency of counter-productive effects, history tends to dispel or work against voluntarist or fatalist illusions from which it is difficult for educators and educational research workers to escape.

Analysis of the foregoing phenomena should lead to a better understanding of the degree of uncertainty which surrounds the development of any action. It should be added that uncertainty has its positive side. In the words of the poet René Char, 'could we live without the prospect of the unknown?'.

These various forms of preparation for action are ensured or illuminated by the action of the historian himself. 'The word to make,' wrote B. Croce, 'must be understood in the broadest sense implying creation of the useful, the moral, the work of art or poetry, of any work of whatever kind. In this we include philosophical and historiographical creation.' Thus, by the same token as poetry, historiography fulfils a carthartic function in liberating the historians from the weight of the past. In this connection let us follow Croce's thought more closely:

We are products of the past; we live submerged in a past which presses in on us from all sides. How can we progress towards a new life, how can we act in a really new way without proceeding out of the past, without raising ourselves above it? And how can we raise ourselves above the past so long as we dwell in it, so long as we are mingled with it? There is only one way out: that of thought. Thought does not break off the relation which unites us with the past; it rises above it in the element of the ideal, transforming it into the known. We have to look at the past from outside it, or – and this is no simple metaphor – turn it into a mental problem and find a solution rich in truth. This solution will be the ideal step through which we can take a new pace forward towards an action, a life truly our own . . . Goethe says somewhere that writing history is a way of setting down the burdens of the past. Historical thought lowers the past to the point of making it into the matter on which it works; it transfigures the past in so doing; and thus historiography liberates us from history[8].

This liberating, carthartic function of historiography should render the individual better able to assume the burden of the present. Can this function be integrated with the goals of the teaching of history?

History as made and as taught

When the purposes of teaching history are formulated in very general terms, historians and teachers subscribe to them without any difficulty. How could one fail to agree with Febvre when he says that the function of history is 'to produce people who know their precise place in the double network of the generations which made them as they are and of the countries of the world around them which exert pressure on, compete with or back up the one in which they live'? Similarly, it would be difficult to disagree with the instructions issued in 1978 by the French Ministry of Education concerning the aims of teaching history in colleges. According to these instructions, the object is, among other things, to develop in the pupils 'a sense of the complexity of social phenomena . . . the sense and pace of evolution in time . . . the sense of geographical diversity . . . the capacity to use acquired ideas and skills in the fulfilment of their responsibilities as consumers, future producers and future citizens . . .'[9].

However, any measure intended to modify the status of history in schools, for example as regards hours, programme or examinations, provokes lively controversy among teachers and research workers. The following are among the disputed questions: whether the general concept of history should be total or sectorial; particular subjects of teaching such as how to take social realities into account; content (i.e. history as it is and as it is taught); methods taking into account the interests and possibilities of pupils; and means, such as the organization of documentation.

The disagreements between historians and teachers also reveal the diversity of schoolbooks not only in different parts of the world but also within the same country. However, this diversity cannot conceal the persistence, in spite of the development of research and the ensuing attempts to bring about reform, of a common characteristic, namely that school history books are usually designed to convey a political point of view presented in the form of a continuous narrative from early times to our own days. In this connection, D. Julia has written that the teaching of history in France has for three centuries continued to observe the principles of its founders. Through the exploitation of examples taken from past centuries, these principles make of it an instrument of moral and political education[10].

On the basis of their school history books, M. Ferro has investigated the images which certain countries make of their past. Apart from its scientific vocation, he considers that history is used as a vehicle for both militant and therapeutic purposes. With regard to the first, he speaks of a 'missionary' history which projects the problems of its own time on to those of the period with which it is ostensibly supposed to be dealing. Thus, for example, under the pressure of events, schools in the United States have changed from the ideology of the 'melting pot' to that of the 'salad bowl', where each culture retains its own identity. Regarding the therapeutic function, a good example is to be found in African countries where 'children's books glorify the great empires of the African past, whose splendour is contrasted with the decadence and backwardness of feudal Europe'[11].

The influence of schoolbooks must not be considered in isolation. There exist other sources of historical culture. Parallel to the institutional history of the schoolbooks which express or justify some ideological or political point of view, there exists an institutional 'counter-history' conveying the aspirations of subjugated groups, and also the 'communal memory', a source lacking specialized agents, frequently confusing myth with history, and using unwritten forms of expression such as religious festivals, epic tales and drama.

These three sources coexist in a peculiar way in ex-colonial countries. In black Africa, for example, 'knowledge of the past is the result of stratification at three levels', according to Ferro. 'The most deeply rooted, namely the oral tradition, is not concerned only with fact but also with myth . . . The second layer is that of history as taught by the colonizing power. Finally, since independence, the impulsion given by African historians and contemporary Africanists has resulted in a general re-evaluation of African history which is still going on'[12].

The occasional contradictions between the messages emanating from these three sources may compromise the political function of teaching history in schools. In every country, the content of such lessons is strongly influenced by the particularities of national history and by the needs of the present time. Thus, at the beginnings of the Third Republic, two contrasting histories were taught in the schools of France, namely lay and Catholic history. In the case of the former, the choice of the French Revolution as the basis of its mythology turns that event into a culminating point. In other words, while the authors of the lay history books considered that revolutions had once been necessary, they took the view that at the end of the nineteenth century this was no longer the case. In this way social antagonisms were papered over in the cause of national unity. For the Catholic authors, any popular uprising against the authorities was to be condemned. Moreover, to the extent that the crisis of modern society was imputed to the weakening of religious sentiment, the Middle Ages became by contrast a sort of golden age. While continuing to argue and criticize each other incessantly, these two historiographies had certain ideals in common which confirm the political function of history teaching: national unity, defence of the national frontiers and the propagation of French civilization by means of colonial expansion[13]. In his *Histoire de l'education populaire en France*[14], the present author demonstrated, in this connection, that the competition between lay and Catholic adult education associations sometimes brought about both standardization and innovation.

In the countries of the Maghreb, the renewal of historiography consists not so much of calling into question the political narrative itself as in suggesting new chronological bearings, a new way of stressing the course of history. Thus, 'in Arabo-Islamic history, the great period of discovery which Western tradition associates with the voyages of Magellan and Christopher Columbus is seen as part of a continuous story from the time of the Venetian explorations down to those of the Arabs in the Indian Ocean, whose geographical and scientific discoveries made possible those of the Genoans and the Venetians'[15]. Similarly, the rewriting of colonial historiography is less concerned with the events themselves than with the significance imputed to them. For example, far from being associated with the desert and with plunder as in the French tradition, the nomadic life is associated with liberty and commerce between cities. In the same way, predominance of the tribe is not seen as constituting an elementary stage of political organization but rather as a form of institutional fall-back in the face of foreign occupation[16].

In Nazi Germany, while school history books were directly based on *Mein Kampf*, the innovation of teaching history in a 'regressive' way, i.e. in starting from the present and going back into time, had a political and apologetic significance. The object was to present Hitler as a hero, the first in the 'regressive' order of things, a combination of history[17].

This review of the pictures which the history books of different countries paint of the past has led Ferro to call the idea of the unity of history into

question and to ask 'if the idea that one version of history is truer than
another is true in itself'. He adds that the challenging of the versions presented in school history books 'in no way means that they should not be
read; for they are the stuff of our identity, our beliefs'[18]. Ferro thus brings
out one of the major contradictions with which any school history programme
must come to terms.

One may put Ferro's reflections into perspective by remembering that history as taught in schools cannot be assimilated to that written by genuine
historians. Moreover, the will to detect and correct mistakes and tendentious
interpretations to which Ferro's work bears witness shows that progress towards greater objectivity is possible. Is not that recognition of diversity and
variability which characterizes the filtration of facts and their relative importance a precondition for the confrontation of points of view and the creation of greater international understanding? Ferro himself suggests a prom-
ising line when he draws a distinction 'between history, which one creates by
means of analysis, and the knowledge which one must possess in order to
analyse something'[19].

This reflection leads us to offer the following comments and suggestions
regarding the goals, content and methods of teaching the history of education:

— In the first place, the history of education should interest the students as
    much as the lecturers. It can supply the former with a choice of motivat-
    ing subjects which can help them to understand their place in the aca-
    demic universe and to assume the new responsibilities stemming from the
    democratization of schools, for example the election of delegates, partici-
    pation in class councils, the management of cultural centres, and so on.
    At the same time it can help lecturers by casting light on current educa-
    tional situations and by providing a sense of proportion with respect to
    educational fashions and excessive enthusiasm. In both cases it can per-
    form what Croce called the 'cathartic' function of liberation from the
    weight of the past. It should be added that the development of this func-
    tion would raise the level of hopes and questions concerning the history
    of education, thus contributing to the progress of this discipline.
— From the point of view of content, a balance should be sought between
    national and local history on the one hand, and, on the other, historical
    analysis of the same problem within the framework of different countries.
    Room should also be found in the programme to mention the 'traps'
    which threaten the writing and interpretation of history: for example, the
    phenomena of projection and recovery stemming from a 'presentist' atti-
    tude; the tendency to reduce current problems to their simple historical
    dimensions; the illusion of immutability, of identicality ('everything has
    already been said'), of the new and unpublished and so on.
— In the history of education, as in other disciplines, it would be well to

bring teaching and research methods closer together. In saying this we are thinking of the analysis of documents, study of the mechanisms and factors of change, and the attempt to identify continuities and specificities by means of continual cross-referencing between the present and the past.

— The development of courses in the history of education calls, among other things, for the meeting of various specialists such as historians, psychologists and sociologists, who would jointly tackle interdisciplinary subjects such as the arousing of interest in history, instilling the sense of time and, more generally, how to ensure that students acquire a scientific attitude[20].

The solutions to these problems will depend, to a large extent, on the existence of a desire constantly to redefine the goals of the teaching of history.

In this connection it would be timely, according to Ferro, to ask ourselves certain questions regarding the causes of the present crisis in this branch of teaching. Among these causes he draws our attention to the following:

— the bankruptcy of ideologies, the effect of which is to cast doubt on any discussion of history;
— changes in the world, particularly since decolonization, which have brought about a less Eurocentric interpretation of history;
— the increase in non-scholastic forms of conveying historical culture, for example films, novels and comic strips;
— the calling into question of traditional styles of history, for example institutional or event oriented, and the onset of societal analysis; and
— the confusion felt by teachers in attempting to render the present time intelligible.

At the end of this analysis, Ferro stresses the following goals for the teaching of history:

— to convey a knowledge of the major events and problems of the nation's history;
— to inculcate an understanding of other societies;
— to work towards an overall intelligibility of the phenomena of the past, as for example in the relations between the destiny of individuals and the general course of history;
— to identify in the past what has ended and what survives, the breaks and the continuities; and
— to give everyone the ability to carry out for himself or herself a reasoned analysis of historical phenomena thanks to a practical understanding of the methods of different human sciences such as demography, economics, anthropology and so on.

Over and above these goals and methods, we should take into account the meaning which historians, educators and also students attribute to history.

NOTES AND REFERENCES

1. Brickman, W.W. Theoretical and critical perspectives on educational history. *Paedagogica historica* (Ghent, Belgium), vol. XVIII, no. 1, 1978, p. 42–83.
2. Carbonell, C.-O. *L'historiographie*. Paris, Presses universitaires de France, 1981. 128 p.
3. Letters to *Le Monde:* L'enseignement de l'histoire. La perte de la mémoire collective, extracts from a letter by P. Eveno. *Le Monde* (Paris), 23 septembre 1983, p. 2.
4. Croce, B. *L'histoire comme pensée et comme action*. 3rd ed. Geneva, Librairie Droz, 1968. 292 p.
5. Brickman, W.W. *Op. cit.*
6. Léon, A. *Introduction à l'histoire des faits éducatifs*. Paris, Presses universitaires de France, 1980. 248 p.
7. Storr, R. The role of education in American history. *Harvard educational review* (Cambridge, MA), vol. 46, no. 3, August 1976, p. 354.
8. Croce, B. *Op. cit.*
9. Léon, A. *Op. cit.*
10. Julia, D. Enseignement de l'histoire. *In:* Le Goff, J., ed. *La nouvelle histoire*. Paris, Retz, 1978, p. 160–165.
11. Ferro, M. *Comment on raconte l'histoire aux enfants à travers le monde entier*. Paris, Payot, 1981, p. 9.
12. Ibid., p. 33.
13. Julia, D. Enseignement de l'histoire. *In:* Le Goff, J., ed. *Op. cit.* p. 165.
14. Léon, A. *Histoire de l'éducation populaire en France*. Paris, Nathan, 1983.
15. Ferro, M. *Op. cit.*, p. 78.
16. Ibid., p. 102.
17. Ibid., p. 129–130.
18. Ferro, M. L'unité de l'histoire en cause? *L'école et la nation* (Paris, Parti communiste français), no. 327, mars 1982, p. 37–38.
19. Ibid., p. 38.
20. Léon, A. *Introduction à l'histoire des faits éducatifs*. Paris, Presses universitaires de France, 1980. 248 p.

Reflections on the meaning of the history of education

The meaning which one gives to the history of education is indissolubly bound to that which one gives to history in general, to the future of humanity and, on another time scale, to individual existence.

More precisely, to discover the meaning of history is to conceive at the same time the possibility of shaping it notably, as was believed in the eighteenth century, thanks to the development of education and culture. Furthermore, the notion of the 'meaning of history' represents the point of convergence, the support for the aspirations, hopes and anxieties of the present time: a need for internal coherence and solidarity, the feeling of malaise or powerlessness in face of the complexity of economic, demographic, cultural and other problems. This all amounts to saying that the supposed direction of history, one's attitudes to the past and future, are a function of the way in which one perceives and experiences the present.

Thus the direction attributed to history, like an interest in the subject or the decision to write it, is historically determined. As Ariès puts it:

In this last third of the twentieth century, we are perhaps witnessing the end of the Light, or at least the end of the belief in the irreversibility and absolute beneficence of scientific and technical progress. Certainly not the end of progress, but the end of the religion of progress, of faith in progress. Perhaps this may be simply a short-term reaction to over-rapid and brutal industrialization. The fact remains that criticism of progress has become a popular theme nowadays, particularly among young people; it was transmitted from a reactionary right wing, which had moreover already abandoned it, to a rather ill-defined, muddled but vigorous left. I have the theory that there exists a relationship between the reticences of the 1960s with regard to development, progress and modernity, and the enthusiasm of young historians for the study of pre-industrial societies and their mentality. These historians do not recognize a direction in history. They no longer want to picture earlier societies as steps along the way in a programmed evolution, to the point where they distrust any diachronic view or systematic research into influences received or exerted. In this way the culture they study is almost withdrawn from history and is judged in the way in which ethnologists and structuralists regard the society which they have chosen to examine[1].

The tendency of many experienced historians to suit their subject-matter and style to the criteria of the novel would appear to correspond closely to Ariès' remarks.

Should such changes constrain us to give up any historiographical project intended to perceive the past with greater lucidity and the future with more optimism? Or, on the contrary, is it possible to continue to speak of progress, at least as regards certain aspects of social and professional life, notably in the field of educational action?

The views of individuals on the direction of evolution depend largely on their philosophical options, their beliefs, their commitments and their personal experience, even if certain thinkers such as Marx or Teilhard de Chardin consider that this direction can be discerned by scientific observation of the past and the present[2].

It is not our purpose to draw up a critical inventory of the various teleological doctrines, philosophies of the absurd and other theories which have come into and gone out of fashion one after the other. Rather it is to examine at greater length certain reflections touched on in the last chapter, and to offer some suggestions with a view to making history a means of preparation for action focused on the present and oriented towards the future at one and the same time.

First of all, however, what should we understand by 'the meaning of history'? Let us consider two definitions of this notion.

In the *first case*, an individual or a group draws from an intelligible picture of the past, knowledge of some law of development or an example taken from the work of pioneers, motivations and rules of behaviour with a view to attaining certain goals (for example, a less élitist school system or a more rational method of teaching) which do not necessarily derive from any clear and precise vision of the future of humanity.

At the end of an important work by several authors on the economic and social history of France, J. Bouvier speaks in the following terms of lessons of 'wisdom' and also 'optimism' which one might draw from a knowledge of certain age-old tendencies:
> Over periods counted in centuries, the history of economic growth and social change reveals a continual swinging motion between social frustration and satisfaction . . . Nevertheless, overall satisfactions continued to exist to which we should award the plus sign, signifying that we recognize their objective existence.

A convergence of heterogeneous class and group interests, of attitudes and action in favour of maintaining predominant social balances has existed for nearly two centuries. To say this is not to 'take up a position', but to try and understand earlier developments and the present state of affairs. Should we agree with Pierre Massé, who has recently written: 'It has become clear that society is conflictual in the short term, which is why history is tragic. But in the long term it is all of a piece, which is why the human race has advanced.'?

It follows that the rest of our history remains open. There is no end to the movement of the pendulum. But here historians lay down their pens. Their trade is not to alter the course of events nor to predict the future. They have enough trouble, dear reader, to follow the confused traces of the past[3].

In the *second case*, the meaning of history takes the future into account, evoking the ideas of a humanity evolving in a certain direction towards a certain goal which Teilhard de Chardin has called the point Omega, representing the supreme unity of humanity; and which Marx has called the classless society, a humanity reconciled with itself.

Teilhard's point Omega is defined as an autonomous entity exterior to the universe which it organizes. Humanity turns towards point Omega as the believer turns towards god. Regarding the forecasts, even prophesies, attributed to Marx, in reality these are above all the work of his numerous disciples. The author of *Das Kapital* spent much more of his time on the critical analysis of capitalist society and on ways of combatting its abuses than in sketching the outlines of future society. However, the *Critique of the Programme of Gotha* (1875) does contain a few such outlines, for example the disappearance of the opposition between manual and intellectual work, multidimensional development of the individual, and so on. According to Teilhard, the goal sought by humanity will be attained by a process of complexification, by which he means a transition from dispersal to organization and unification; according to Marx, it will be attained as a result of the contradictions undermining the successive modes of production and of the ensuing social struggle. In both cases, the evolutionary process leads to the triumph of certain values and to individual and collective well-being. In a word, the direction of history is assimilated to the notion of progress.

The educator who follows this definition of the meaning of history is confronted with certain ambiguities. In effect, owing to the awareness which it occasions and the means which it supplies, education tends to accelerate the evolutionary process. But the 'course of history' may also lead to fatalistic attitudes when it is endowed with the prophetic properties specifying stages by which humanity cannot help but pass in order to attain some precisely defined goal.

It goes without saying that this second view is not tenable if the 'necessary' yields to the 'possible' or even the 'probable', and if the action of human beings is considered indispensable to the accomplishment of the historical process. In this connection, Kant holds that the future of a humanity oriented towards the progress of liberty is possible but not certain. His muted optimism is based on the idea that short recurrences of barbarism cannot prevent the transmission of 'the germs of enlightenment' to future generations. He believes that his own philosophical work would render the desired future more probable[4].

In order to be fully convincing and effective, the prophetic concept of history must periodically provide retrospective proofs of the accuracy of its forecasts. If the historian considers these proofs unconvincing, he is obliged to fall back on the first and more limited notion of the course of history.

In fact, the difficulties of prophetic history have given rise to various attempts to define principles and rules drawn from analysis of the past and present, and designed to guide action in the future. In the United States, for example, the theoreticians of 'chaos' imagine the long run as 'a median line resulting from successive balances and imbalances caused by variations in the relation of forces'[5]. In addition, certain 'laws' should provide guidelines for the action of politicians. Among such 'laws' we may note the following:
— 'All empires must perish.'
— 'It is a capital error to imagine that one can sweep away the past.'
— 'Human beings need a sense of identity.'
— 'After scoring a point off a stubborn adversary it is important not to rest on one's laurels, because he will try to make you pay for it sooner or later.'

One might question the scope and scientific nature of these rules, even if the 'chaos' theory embodies the transposition of laws from various fields of physics, notably meteorology. In this connection, we know that chaos has its own laws. For example, the weather is chaotic but in spite of that it never snows in the Sahara in August.

On the Marxist side, the multiplicity of movements which nowadays claim kinship does not prevent certain authors from declaring that 'the universality of the process of human liberation is nothing other than the tendency to a socialist issue to each crisis, each struggle'[6]. As we have seen in Chapter V, other authors reject any universal and prophetic theory of the evolution of humanity. For them, the analysis of social reality with all its contradictions reveals the possibility both of resisting oppression and of experiencing the contrasts between the different aspects of life. These authors also consider that all change is ambiguous since it can lead at the same time to progress in one place and regression in another[7].

Social and educational reality provides many examples of this ambiguity. For example, we may think of the effects of generalizing secondary education or the consequences of transferring advanced technology to certain Third World countries.

The extent and complexity of the effects attributable to any change force us to limit the field or subject regarding which it would be possible to speak of a purely positive or negative outcome. Let us take as an example the working conditions of lecturers in teachers' training colleges in France at the beginning of the twentieth century:

The internal service regulations of the ladies primary teachers' training colleges are so narrow and hard on the personnel that they appear to come from another century. The lecturers must invigilate the dormitories, studies, religious services and walks. If rain rules out the possibility of taking a walk, they then have to amuse a large troop of girls whose life in the hall of residence is heavy and boring . . . The students must be escorted to the baths, to the dentist, to the station . . . There must be surveillance 24 hours a day . . . A wife and mother dwelling in the town may be obliged to spend part of her nights invigilating the dormitories . . . we are governed by the arbitrary means of our directors who do not even ask us with what sauce we want to be devoured . . . For supervisors and students alike, this is not so much a boarding institution as a prison camp[8].

In the light of the foregoing, can one deny that conditions have noticeably improved during the course of the present century? It would be good to have room here to recall the struggles and stages which led to this evolution.

However that may be, this example enables us to speak of a direction of history or, more precisely, of a sense of observed change, as long as the subjects chosen are relatively well defined as in the case, for example, of the situations of teachers or pupils, programme content, teaching methods, the working day and free time of factory workers, and so on.

The evaluation of observed change, like any attempt to understand the past, presupposes the existence of a frame of reference common, or at least partly so, to the different periods under consideration. In other words, the values of dignity, freedom and justice, to which the teachers at the beginning of the century implicitly referred, continue to inspire the debates and conflicts of our own time. In a general way, one of the functions of historical enquiry is to draw attention to the coexistence of 'sameness' and 'otherness' in the relationship between past and present.

Even when the field of research is very limited, progress is not always seen as linear. It may be charactized by an apparent return to older ideas and practices. One might mention, for example, the Gardner Report recently published by the United States Department of Education. After listing the sources of the decline in the level of achievement in schools, the report proposes, among other things, a considerable increase in the length of the school day and the obligation for secondary school pupils to study at least five basic subjects.

In the field of teaching, it is usual to perceive a progress from what are called 'passive' to 'active' methods, and behaviourist or Piagetian concepts are adduced as evidence for this view. However, in delving into what he calls social apprenticeship, A. Bandura has shown the importance of substitution processes. In other words, the acquisition of knowledge and skills is not necessarily the result of the individual's own efforts or his estimate of the results of his efforts. Both children and adults acquire a good deal of motor and cognitive behaviour by observing the actions of others and their results[9]. Should we not therefore consider as progress this new awareness of the possibilities offered by social apprenticeship?

As to the future, observation of the recent past would lead us to greet the speculations of futurologists or even the simple extrapolation of empirical regularities with some circumspection. It would also tend to provoke an attitude of mistrust regarding the systematic criticism of what are considered to be traditional patterns, particularly when such criticism is expressed in incantatory terms where pedagogical verbiage and political literary vocabulary are combined in an excessive use of fashionable formulae such as 'knowing when to change', 'learning to be', 'learning to become', 'knowing how to adapt', or 'foreseeing the unforeseeable'.

In the face of certain speculations about the future, history warns us against the illusion that the education system works independently and linearly. It is a truism to recall that the system evolves as a result of conditions in the past and various elements of the present, notably the action of those holding political office. But at the same time we also know that the effects of such action partly escape the comprehension or the control of those who initiate it.

Thus the forms and orientations of education in the future necessarily remain an open question. In helping us to find answers, historical thought can only turn us towards a more complete and rigorous analysis of the present, in other words towards better preparation for the future.

Nevertheless, a fundamental problem remains. Can the individual give an orientation to the history of education without at the same time giving one to his own activity as a teacher or research worker, without affirming his hope in humankind, without believing in progress, in the possibility of improving the structures and the working of any education system?

For those who do not subscribe to any system of belief or who do not expect historical research to support or confirm established truths, might it not be possible to envisage a relative concept of the meaning of history? In this case, discerning a historical direction in a given cultural or political area would involve a double process. On the one hand, it would be necessary to work out, on the basis of explicit criteria, a critical balance sheet of the progress achieved in each branch of the education system, and, on the other, to imagine future goals for action and research stemming from the most thorough analysis of the requirements and possibilities of our own time.

NOTES AND REFERENCES

1. Ariès, P. L'histoire des mentalités. *In:* Le Goff, J., ed. *La nouvelle histoire.* Paris, Retz, 1978, p. 411.
2. Teilhard de Chardin, P. *La place de l'homme dans la nature.* Paris, Union générale d'édition, 1962.
3. Braudel, F.; Labrousse, E.; Bouvier, J. *Histoire économique et sociale de la France.* Paris, Presses universitaires de France, 1982, t. IV, p. 1739–1740.

4. Veyne, P. *Comment on écrit l'histoire.* Paris, Seuil, 1978.
5. Fontaine, A. Des lois pour le chaos? *Le Monde* (Paris), 24 juillet 1983.
6. Michaux, B. Le marxisme du 21ᵉ siècle. *L'école et la nation* (Paris, Parti communiste français), no. 337, mars 1983, p. 38.
7. Gaudeau, J.; Naud, D. Marxisme et progrès. *Raison présente* (Paris), no. 66, 1983, p. 83–95.
8. *Bulletin trimestriel de l'Association amicale des professeurs des écoles normales d'instituteurs et des écoles normales d'institutrices de France,* no. 1, 1903, p. 13–51.
9. Bandura, A. *Social learning theory.* Englewood Cliffs, NJ, Prentice-Hall, 1977.

APPENDIX

Note on the International Association for the History of Education

In Chapter II we mentioned the activities of several centres of research on the history of education.

The enquiry from which we derived this information could only cover a very limited number of institutions. Since we lack space to provide an adequately representative sample of bodies engaged in research, we will simply offer the reader a few useful references to national officials or correspondents of the International Association for the History of Education.

This information is taken from the Association's *International newsletter for the history of education*, the aims of which were referred to in the introduction to this book.

A. *Members of the executive committee of the association*

Prof. Maurits de Vroede, *president*, Université catholique, Vessalius straat 2, B-3000 Louvain (Belgium).

Pierre Gaspard, Institut national de recherche pédagogique, 29, rue d'Ulm, 75005 Paris (France).

Prof. Giovanni Genovesi, University of Parma, Via Passo della Chisa 23, 43100 Parma (Italy).

Prof. Manfred Heinemann, University of Hanover, Lüerstr. 3, D-3000 Hanover (Federal Republic of Germany).

Prof. Jurgen Herbst, University of Wisconsin, 1000 Bascom Mall, Madison, WI 53706 (United States).

Prof. James Lynch, Faculty of Education, Hammerton Hall, 4 Gray Road, Sunderland SR2 7EE (United Kingdom).

Prof. Kadriy Salimova, Scientific Research Institute of General Pedagogics, Ulitsa Pavla Korchagina 7, Moscow 129278 (USSR).

Prof. Otto Vág, Lágymáosi, U-12, 1111 Budapest (Hungary).

B. *Members of the editorial committee of the association's newsletter*

The chief editor of the *Newsletter* is Professor Manfred Heinemann of the University of Hanover (see above).

Various countries are represented on the editorial committee by the following persons:

Australia and New Zealand: Dr M.M. Pawsey, Victoria College, Burwood Campus, Burwood, Victoria 3125.

Austria: Prof. T. Gönner, Franziskanergasse, 1, A-5025 Salzburg.

Belgium and the Netherlands: Prof. K. De Clerk, Centre pour l'étude de l'histoire de l'éducation, A. Baertsoenkaai 3, B-9000 Ghent.

Canada: Prof. W. Bruneau, Faculty of Education, University of British Columbia, Vancouver, B.C. V6T 1W5.

France: P. Gaspard (see above).

Federal Republic of Germany: Prof. M. Heinemann (see above).

Hungary: Prof. O. Vág (see above).

Iran: Prof. F. Bazargan, University of Tehran, Tehran.

Israel: Prof. A.F. Kleinberger, University of Tel-Aviv, School of Education, Ramat-Aviv, Tel-Aviv.

Italy: L. Bellatalla, Via Italo Possenti 26, I-56100 Pisa.

Mexico: Dr J. Vazques, College of Mexico, Las Flores 499-2, Mexico.

Norway: Prof. ass. O. Sunnana, Pedagogisk Forskningsistitutt, P.O.B. 1092, Blindern, N-Oslo.

Poland: J. Dybiec, ul. Kliny 4/14, 31-465, Cracow.

Spain: Prof. J.R. Berrio, Département d'histoire de l'éducation, Coslada, 7, Madrid 28.

Switzerland: Prof. F.P. Hager, Institut pédagogique de l'université de Zürich, Rämistr. 71, CH-8006 Zürich.

United Kingdom: Dr P. Cunningham, College of Westminster, North-Hinkse, Oxford OX2 9AT.

United States: M.S. Shereshewsky, Newsletter of the History of Education Society, 38 N. Cottage Place, Westfield, New Jersey 07090.

WITHDRAWN
FROM STOCK

WITHDRAWN
FROM STOCK